Table of

9 Truths Every Boy Should Know About Masculinity

Find Purpose, Exercise Mindfulness, and Reach Your Truest Potential as a Man

Matt Winters

Introduction

Boys will always be boys? No, not really. Boys will always be what their fathers, mothers, leaders, and society say they should be, and boy, there has never been a time when the voices were competing for a say in the matter more than now. Everyone has their own definition of masculinity, trying to define what men should be like in terms that fit their world and their agenda. It's no wonder so many young men are confused about what they are supposed to do or who they are supposed to be. I was confused at some point, and you might be too.

Well, don't worry. While it's true that you are living in a confused world during confusing times, this does not mean you cannot find your footing and have your say in how your life goes. You have already started to define your own life by reading this book, taking the time to block out all those opinions about who you should be, and trying to find a single truth to frame your life around. That truth actually comes in nine parts and will take you on a journey from the boy you are now to the man you need to be to bring change to your own life and the lives of the people around you. Congratulations on getting started!

I have always been fascinated by two groups of boys in literature: the lost boys from *Peter Pan* and the little boys from Pinocchio's story. I always found it funny that both groups of boys refused to grow into the men they needed to be and the type of men that the communities they lived in needed in order to thrive. The result was them living in a sort of exile away from society and everyone else. I have a great fear that this phenomenon has left the Disney studios and is now becoming a reality in our world. We have many young boys who are failing to grow up and become men, and because of this, they are becoming a segregated and outcast group who think they can do what they want.

Now there might not be a physical island where they gather and reinforce the toxic behaviors they refuse to let go of, but the internet has given them a platform to do so and do so effectively. Communities like the incel groups and other outcast groups of men have risen online and are recruiting young boys by the dozen.

According to Blake and Brooks (2022):

Involuntarily celibate men ('incels') commonly advocate for societal disruption, including violence toward women. Their anger can make them susceptible to radicalization, revolution, or reactionary hostility. Research efforts aimed at identifying the causes and consequences of incels' beliefs are needed to address this growing problem.

Unfortunately, since they do not really know what they are supposed to do with their lives or what they should be, these young men become whatever seems expedient and fun instead of chasing meaning and growth.

Not you though, and not your son or friend. That is not the path designed for you. I know so many people who have almost gone down that very same path, and I know you do not want to. There is so much isolation, rejection, and fear in that state that you will not be able to stay mentally healthy there or grow in any way. I have spoken to countless boys and men about what makes a real man and have used all these views and experiences—mixed with lots of research—to extract the fundamentals of being a real man.

The confusion, though, is inevitable; we live in a world that is constantly changing and evolving, and that has had a significant effect on the setup of social structures. That, plus the interweaving of cultures through the increase in globalization, and you get yourself a concoction for confusion. It's not your fault if you do not know how to properly orient yourself in the world, but it's your absolute responsibility to find a way out and grow into the man that your community needs—not wants, but needs. You are meant to be an agent of growth, progress, harmony, and development for yourself and the people you care about. This should be the framework that guides your ambitions and goals in life, and once you get there, you will be all set.

That's where this book comes in: Here, we will take a journey from where you are to where you should be—from being a boy to being a man. It's just nine simple steps, but they're enough to get you through the door. You can see this book as a guide and a friend as you journey to discover what it really means to be a man in the modern world and how you can become one. Are you ready for the journey? I know I am; I know where this journey will lead you, and I am excited for you to get there. Strap in, soldier, the journey has just begun.

First Truth: Masculinity Is Just One Facet of Being a Man, Not the Entirety of It

Masculinity is often equated to being a man, almost as if being masculine is the entirety of being a man, the only determining factor for how much of a man you actually are. It becomes even more convoluted when the definition of masculinity is not clear or healthy for young men and boys who are trying to find their places in the world.

In this chapter, we will discuss how there is so much more to being a man besides masculinity. Or more precisely, we will redefine masculinity so you can have the full picture of what it really is. This is a good place to start because it's the root of all nine of the truths; if you do not understand what masculinity is or what it means to be a man, then you will have a very hard time understanding the rest of the truths in the book. Now let's start off by addressing the greatest threat to your manhood—toxic masculinity.

What Is "Toxic" Masculinity?

It is difficult to define toxic masculinity in a single line, or even a paragraph. It's such a complex concept that manifests differently in different people, but there are subtle similarities you can pick out that will help you identify it within yourself and others. There are three common traits I have noticed in people who have a toxic masculinity complex running through their veins: suppression of emotions, dominance, and aggression.

Maybe as you read those three phrases, you identified them as what you thought true masculinity should be, and that's okay—most people do think masculinity is those things. Have you ever heard anyone say, "Real men don't cry," "Real men don't get told what to do," or "Real men fight for themselves and others when they have been provoked"? Because we hear these types of things so often, our minds are used to these ideas, and we internalize them without even realizing it.

Suppression of emotion comes from the notion that because men are strong, they should not cry or show emotion. This belief, however, leads to instability and some serious mental health problems for a lot of young men. We will go over how this plays out more in the later parts of this chapter, but when you allow emotions to brew inside instead of letting them out, they become a poison to your body and your mind. All of that pent-up emotion will eventually make its way out in the form of dominance and aggression.

It's okay to be dominant sometimes, and there is nothing wrong with being assertive and taking dominion in a situation where it's appropriate and you have the opportunity to do so. True dominance is taking charge when things are chaotic and bringing order to your life and the lives of the people around you. However, most guys think that being a dominant man means controlling others and taking the light away from other people's lives and making it their own. Do not fall into that trap. Dominance with the purpose of subduing others is toxic and not how you want to live.

So now you have emotions that are just pent up inside of you, and you also have a need to move into other people's space and demand respect and honor. What do you think that will lead to? Yes, aggression. When society tells young people to bottle up their emotions, they become emotionally volatile and entitled, spilling their hate into the world later in life. That is what toxic masculinity really is: Men who do not know how to deal with their emotions and who prey on everyone else around them in an attempt to gather power and praise for themselves so they can feel better.

The sad part is that people do not tell young men how harmful this can be to their lives. We all know and see how much toxic masculinity affects other people, but we need to also see and address how much it affects the men themselves. It becomes a vicious cycle if it is not addressed properly. As a young man, you need to know what these effects are and how they will impact you. Though masculinity will help you as you orient yourself in the world, it is also good to be aware of the traits you don't want to take on as you develop your own masculinity.

The biggest and most dangerous side effect you might experience due to toxic masculinity is how it affects your mental health. This comes in two ways: the increasing mental weight of unattended emotions and seeing the world through unhealthy filters. This adds strain to your relationships, misdirects your ambitions, and gives you unhealthy expectations for what life is supposed to be like. Again, the loop keeps getting bigger and feeding into itself until you are trapped and cannot escape to find your true self.

Media and Stereotypes

I cannot emphasize enough just how much of a role the media has played in reinforcing these toxic masculinity traits. Every now and then, there is a show or movie that tries to embrace the very poisonous ideas we are trying to keep from taking over our minds. To be honest, it is not easy to distinguish between the propaganda that the media tries to push and the path of healthy masculinity. What you can do is understand how the media works to push and reinforce these ideas and develop mental blocks that will help keep you from internalizing them.

The main tool that the media uses is the perpetuation of stereotypes. By showing you the stereotypes over and over in the content you consume, you will be less able to discern between the toxic structures and the healthy ones. The media perpetuates the traditional representations of manhood that are defined by a need for dominance, denying one's emotions, and hyper-aggression. Many movies show men as being strong, combative warriors who should win every battle and take over wherever they go.

The men portrayed in these movies and shows do not appear to have emotions or they seem to not have to deal with their emotions at all. When the heroes are robotic and never show a sign of weakness, we start to aspire to that. So how can you block out all these stereotypes and continue to build yourself into a real man? Well, the only way you can tell a fake from an original is by knowing the original very well.

There will always be multiple versions of the fake, and you will never be able to tell all of them apart from the original—except if you are deeply familiar with the original. Once you understand what it really means to be a man, you will not have to worry about what the media and the rest of the internet throw at you. If it is not the truth and does not set you up for a meaningful life, then we will do away with it.

While we started with what toxic masculinity is, most of this book will focus more on defining and finding true masculinity. It's not the lies that we are going to discuss but the truths that can lead us to become better husbands, fathers, brothers, and members of the communities we live in. By the end of the book, you will not only know what it means to be a real man but also how to become one. This journey is not only for knowledge but for transformation as well. That's what truth does: It changes the status quo, and it changes the people, the person—you, in this case.

One challenge that I have for you is to make an effort to find and follow inspirational people who reinforce the truths that you are about to learn. If you find people both in your life and in the media who embody what you are aiming to become, you can put effort into emulating them and doing everything you can to learn from them.

Social Expectations

Society will have its own definitions of what you should be like, and sometimes these social boxes are good and safe, but not always. It's tough when you are in social situations that make you feel pressured to embody the very aspects of masculinity you know to be wrong. I remember this being a prevalent problem in college, where it was common to hear people say things like "If you don't do this or that, you are not a real man." These influences promote a lifestyle of aggression and dominance, which won't do any good for boys or their communities.

I remember a time when I saw a guy run nude across the field at night in the rain just to prove he was brave and wouldn't back down from a dare. We hear of such incidents and fail to realize that, while stories like this one are less common, they show us what is actually happening at the subconscious level when a society lies to boys. They take these lies and dare themselves to live up to those challenges.

Society thinks that boys should be able to fight. Okay then, the boys will get into fights, even when they do not need to, and may even end up being violent toward their wives and children in the future. Society thinks men should not address their emotions. Okay then, young men will pretend they are okay until the pressure breaks them down and ruins their mental health.

Even in cases when the dare seems to be something good, like calling boys forth to be men or to step up and take responsibility, society can still unknowingly harm you. You are not meant to carry the weight of the world on your shoulders—you could not do it even if you tried. Unfortunately, society will sometimes demand a lot from you. When this happens, you should know it's not on you to solve every problem, but you can work to resolve as many as you can.

It's not only society that is imposing these toxic gender norms on our boys and men, but sometimes it's the education system and even parents who push these views too. Therefore, everyone has a part to play in changing the narrative and in sharing these truths with the men of our era. Most importantly, every guy has a responsibility to rise up and not only believe these truths but live them out.

Breaking Stereotypes

So what can you do to break the stereotypes that are being upheld by the media and community you live in? Is there anything you can actually do to break these stereotypes in the first place? Yes and no; you cannot single-handedly remove the entire narrative from existence, but you can remove it from your own life. Maybe if you do that well enough, you can influence some people around you, and that influence can bring some level of freedom from the stereotypes all around.

If you focus on removing the stereotypes altogether, then you have already lost the war. The real battle is making sure that they do not have a hold on you and that you are free from their influence. You can never eradicate a way of thinking that has been so widely influential for so long. The best you can do is what you are doing right now: seek out the truth and learn to embody it.

Another way to deal with and break stereotypes is by going directly against them as hard as you can. Think about it: If you go against the stereotype with all that you are, then you are basically training yourself to become the opposite of what it says. The next time you are feeling sad, take time to feel the emotions and process them. Cry if you need to and let it all out. See how it feels to be vulnerable and actually deal with your emotions instead of just brushing them off. Another way to break the stereotypes is to try to intentionally stay away from aggression and choose to be more levelheaded and calmer in tense situations to prove that responding aggressively has no bearing on how much of a man you really are.

Positive Aspects of Masculinity

We have mentioned that there are a lot of positive aspects to masculinity that must be kept, so let's go over what some of those are. We should never throw the baby out with the bathwater because masculinity has been beneficial to the world in many ways, and it's important to understand how it can be useful to individuals and society so you can differentiate between the positive aspects and the toxic ones.

Strength and Resilience

The first aspect of masculinity is strength and resilience—a man's ability to remain brave and push through hard times with confidence and courage. This is the backbone of civilization as many of the things we enjoy have been built on the backs of men who chose to keep working until they found the solutions that were needed by their communities at the time. This is something you will need to apply to your ambitions; be strong and unwavering in your pursuit of the meaningful.

Being strong and resilient should be applied in three areas of life: physical strength, emotional strength, and mental strength. I know when people hear "strength" and "masculinity" in the same sentence, they immediately start thinking of muscles and wrestling. While it is great to be able to defend yourself physically when you need to, it's not all the strength you need as a man. In addition to that, if you have physical strength, you should not misuse it by using it to harm the people you should protect.

In addition to being physically strong, you will need to be emotionally strong. Emotional strength is not the same as ignoring your emotions—something many young men do. If you ignore your emotions, they will remain, and they will affect your life down the road. Bottled-up negative emotions become a poison that can lead to emotional stress and even outbursts. Being able to face your emotions and deal with them in a healthy way instead of pushing them down or running away when things get hard is what it really means to be emotionally strong as a man.

Lastly, you want to be mentally strong as well. This is where resilience comes in—the ability to mentally commit and push yourself to make things happen, even when challenges get in the way. You will need to have strong ambition and determination if you are going to make anything happen. It's that desire to see results that will keep you going and turn you into a man who makes change happen for himself, his loved ones, and the rest of the world. Think about it: If you have physical and emotional strength but no motivation to push for anything, then what good are they?

Leadership and Empowerment

Another aspect of masculinity that will help you position yourself for success is the ability to lead and empower the people around you. A boy is dependent on the decisions of others and cannot make decisions for himself; he needs the approval of other people because that is how he gets a sense of empowerment. However, when you grow to become a man, it turns into the opposite; you will need to learn to make decisions that will help the people around you and be the one who empowers others.

A hallmark of positive masculinity is the ability to lift others up and not need to have all the glory all the time. You will need to nurture this within yourself. It takes time, but you can start now. Every time you are out with friends, ask yourself what you can do to make someone else feel empowered and supported and how you can share glory with someone else.

Protecting and Nurturing

I have always found this one idea from superhero movies intriguing. The question is what makes a superhero? It certainly isn't strength because the villain always has their fair share of that too. It's not age, gender, wealth, or even compliance with the law. Think about it: When we see vigilantes, we do not see them as villains, but instead, we root for them and support them like we would the "heroes." Why is that? I think the common trait we see is the willingness to help, protect, and nurture those who are weaker than the heroes themselves.

That is what it really means to be a hero—you have to be willing to use your strength and abilities to protect others, even and especially when you are not getting any recognition for it. Being a hero is the ultimate personification of being a man. This means true masculinity chooses to help and protect others, regardless of what they get in return and how it will impact them in the end. It's a selfless position that will have you putting others first in everything you do, but it will also give you gratification when you see the joy and growth in others because of you.

You don't have to go out and fight crime at night to protect the people around you. You can start by standing up with and for the groups in your community that need your help. Sometimes that looks like holding yourself back from being the cause of pain for another person or group, and from there, you can grow to become a better person.

It will be hard for you to do any of this unless you understand and embrace the fact that masculinity is not the opposite of compassion and empathy. If anything, being a man means understanding and being compassionate and empathetic toward yourself first, then letting that flow over to the people around you.

Redefining Masculinity

All of this comes back to you. How can you apply this to position yourself in life as a force for good? How can you go from being a boy to being the type of man who will lead himself first and then use that discipline to bring change and progress to the world around him? You will have to start by changing how you look at life and reframing how you identify yourself.

You need to redefine what it means to be masculine, and using the truth we just went over, you now know what positive masculinity is and what some of the weaknesses of masculinity are. Leave the toxic and embrace the healthy; establish yourself as the type of boy who seeks personal growth and development and helps others with theirs as well, and the results will be transformative. Now that we have gone over the truth of what masculine strength is, let's move on and talk about the next truth—looking more deeply at the ideas of masculinity and strength.

Second Truth: A Man's Strength Lies Not Only in Physical Power but Also in Emotional Intelligence

Your strength is very important—your physical strength that is—but it is not everything, and it is certainly not enough in itself. You can view your physical strength as similar to the physical components of a computer—the hardware. Just as the camera, display, keyboard, and everything else on a computer are very useful, so is your physical strength; each component helps you get a lot done, and you absolutely need them to be effective and successful in life.

Now imagine how well all those physical components on a computer would work if you did not have the drivers that connect them to the software. It's the drivers and software that make sure the physical components can do what they were made to do, and without those in place, the physical components are completely useless.

This is exactly how it is with you as well. Your physical strength is very important, but you need to have the wisdom to know when and how to responsibly use it for the betterment of your life and those of the people you care about. Your emotional intelligence and your mind are the two components that help you determine how to use your physical energy, making them like your drivers and software in a way.

You can achieve so much when you figure out how to direct and use your energy to improve your life and the world rather than spending it on chasing whatever feels expedient at the time. Your energy is going to be spent on something no matter what, and if you do not plan to intentionally spend it wisely, then you will be bound to the default, which is going wherever the wind takes you.

In this chapter, we will go over how you can maintain your emotional intelligence to keep a balance between your physical strength and how you use it. We will talk about how you can become more aware of your emotions and how that ties in with building a strong character as a man. Your physical strength is not everything about you, and it is not the full essence of being a man. Let's explore the other half and bring the two together.

Emotional Awareness

Emotional awareness is the ability to recognize your emotions and those of the people you are interacting with. You would think that we already do this automatically since we have been feeling emotions since we were born, but that's not actually the case. Emotions are very complex, and they have a very weird relationship with our minds. This is especially true when we are talking about negative emotions, which our minds try to avoid as much as possible.

Let me paint you a picture: Have you ever gotten home from a long day at school or work, and as soon as you get there, you get mad because your younger siblings or your children are running around the house and making noise? You might lash out at them and shout until you see something else that makes you upset and start going off about that. You seem to be finding so many wrong things, things that have probably been like that for a long time but you are only just now noticing.

Well, what probably really happened was something at work or school upset you, such as your boss being disappointed in your work or a friend making a rude comment toward you. In the moment, your brain avoided processing your feelings and you became angry without realizing it. As you then continued through the rest of your day, your mind found other places to direct that anger, like your children or siblings.

Now, if you are emotionally aware, you will be able to recognize when your emotions come into play and where they are coming from. In this case, emotional awareness allows you to acknowledge and manage the emotion when it happens so you can arrive home and be a joy to everyone around you because you are not inappropriately lashing out at them. Now think of it a different way: What if you go to a bar after work and someone bumps into you by mistake, spilling your drink? If you happen to be suppressing some negative emotions, you are likely to get into a physical fight without stopping to think about why you are doing it.

If you are not aware of your emotions, you will become a slave to them and fail to direct your energy appropriately. You need to practice acknowledging your emotions and identifying them accurately. You need to learn to become the master of your emotions and feelings, and then you will be able to direct your energy toward what is meaningful and rewarding.

Beyond recognizing what emotions you are feeling, though, you will need to be able to see the emotions before they hit. You can do this by understanding your emotional triggers. So many boys do not have a clue about what makes them feel angry, ashamed, happy, and all those other emotions in between, and this leaves them vulnerable as the emotions take over without them even noticing. Your triggers are the things that make you feel certain emotions when they happen. These could be words spoken or actions performed by other people that stir up something inside you that has deep-seated meaning from your formative years.

Regardless, if you understand the things that cause these emotions to come alive, then you can actively avoid being in situations where your emotions could get triggered or notice when you are becoming triggered and calm yourself or remove yourself from the situation. This is the beginning of emotional management. You do not need to react to everything that happens around you, at least not on impulse, and you can have a say in what you do and when you do it as long as you have control over your emotions. Let's take a look at what specific actions you can take to regulate and control your emotions instead of blindly following them.

Self-Regulation

Remember, your body and physical strength are like the hardware of a computer, and your emotional state and mind are like the software. Sometimes the hardware of the computer will get hot, and this causes slow speeds and malfunction, so the computer turns on the fans to quickly cool down the hardware whenever the temperature gets too high. It's inevitable that if you use a computer for long enough, especially on demanding tasks, it will need to cool itself down at some point.

As you go through your day and do all these demanding tasks and try to work with all these people, it is also inevitable that at some point, something will happen that will make you emotional. You might not even have an encounter with someone, but the workload itself can make you feel tired, unsure, sad, angry, and a whole load of other emotions. In these situations, you need to turn on your fans and take a moment to cool down.

You can use mindfulness to cool yourself down and prepare yourself to get back on track and chase your ambitions again. Earlier, we talked about how important it is for you to deal with your emotions instead of letting them simmer and then come out later. To build on that, it is actually best to deal with your emotions as soon as they come up instead of dealing with them later because emotions are like little bugs in your mind—they will keep bothering you until you deal with them. Your mind will continue to feel on edge as a way to remind you that you still need to address the emotions that are bothering you. We are going to look at three of my favorite mindfulness techniques that can help you get back on track when you feel yourself getting upset and need to cool off. You can try all of these out to see which one works best for you, and I bet you will find one that blends perfectly with your lifestyle.

Breathing Exercises

It's crazy when you think about how we are breathing every moment of our lives, but sometimes we just need to be aware and intentional in order to do it right. Whenever something happens that makes us emotional or bothered, one of the first areas to be disturbed is our breathing. You will notice your breathing rate increase when you are angry, and you will also sigh more frequently. All of these physical reactions are your body's ways of trying to get enough oxygen so you can deal with the uncertainty that triggered the emotions you're experiencing.

Breathing exercises help you get all the oxygen you need to your head to cool it down. You can see it as turning on a fan for your brain—though the actual internal process is nothing like it. In a way, you are trying to get the right amount of air to keep your temperature regulated, just like a computer will do when it overheats. Now let's look at the simple steps you can take to do a breathing exercise when you need one.

Start off by breathing in through your nose with your mouth sealed tight. Inhale for about seven seconds, allowing your body to get as much of that needed oxygen in as it can. When you have done this, hold your breath for three to four seconds before you let go, and then breathe out for five seconds. Repeat this for another nine rounds to make a total of 10 times and then calm your body.

With your eyes closed—where possible—think about what you need to do to avoid diminishing your mind and energy any further. Think about how you can make your day better and how you can reconcile with anyone who has rubbed you the wrong way. There isn't always a clear answer; sometimes there isn't a good way to get a resolution, and sometimes it's just too early for the resolution to be implemented.

Every now and then, however, you will find a solution as you do the breathing exercise that could save you a lot of time and energy. Even when the solutions to your problems do not become immediately obvious after you have gone through the exercise, you will still have a calm mind and be able to continue with your day as productively as ever. You may even be more productive since the breathing will help you collect yourself in every way and get running again. It's like a reboot—you are shutting down and deleting all the unnecessary tasks from your mind's RAM.

Breathing is one of many ways for you to manage your emotions and reactions, but it's only the doorway to a life of control. You essentially need to learn three skills in order to stay levelheaded all the time, and the breathing exercise goes very well with all three. I want you to use the breathing technique as a guide rather than as the only way to deal with your emotions. You will get into situations where you really do not have time to step away and breathe or think about how to react, so you need to teach your mind to do this even when you are in a stressful situation you can't get yourself out of.

The first thing you will need to learn to do is to understand your emotions and those of others. One of the reasons things escalate is that sometimes people take too long to identify what is really going on, and by the time they do, it's too late. You need to learn how to read cues in the faces and bodies of the people around you. This will give you a good gauge of the emotions in the room or conversation, and you can even prevent situations from erupting by managing them well.

After you realize what is going on, you need to learn to calm down and manage your emotions. Notice I said *manage* your emotions, not *suppress* them; there is a very important distinction between the two. You need to be able to stop yourself from being overtaken by your emotions in the moment so you can manage the situation quickly and effectively. You will still need to acknowledge and deal with how you feel after the fact no matter what.

After you have managed the emotions, then you need to learn to influence the situation. This can be really hard to do, especially if you are not already in charge or don't have a position of power in the situation. However, if you manage your own emotions well, you will realize that other people will look to you for comfort and counsel—that is to say, they will give you the chance to bring your energy into the environment.

I remember the first time I was part of a company that was going to downsize. After the announcement was made, everyone was panicking, including myself. We were all talking about how we should leave before we get fired and how we would make it if we got laid off, cooking up and sharing conspiracies about why and how it would happen. Then there was Walter, one of the guys I worked with.

In all the commotion, Walter stayed calm and never showed panic or fear. In fact, his words were positive and encouraging, talking about how everyone was really talented and how we would all be okay regardless of what happened. You could see that he was very genuine, and you could not help but look forward to hearing him talk. Every time he commented, he gave hope and peace to a situation where it was hard to find any.

That can be you in your own life and to the people around you. It does not necessarily mean things are going well and you do not have a good reason to be upset or worried; it only shows that you understand what is happening and you have mastered how to control your emotions and the energy of the room. To be a man is to be the person who brings their own positivity into a room and shares it with everyone else.

Ask yourself how most people feel after talking to you. Do they walk away feeling more anxious, afraid, paranoid, or unsure about life, or do they tap into some of that peace that you have? How are you intentionally working to make sure you can eventually control your emotions better than you do now? If you do not control your emotions, they will control you. That is not the path you want to go down.

Empowering Vulnerability

There is a recurring theme with this truth, a central idea that is not only integral to understanding it but also to your journey as a man trying to establish yourself in the world. This idea of vulnerability or the ability to accept and face emotions voluntarily so we can become better and stronger than who we are now. You will have to embrace the scars for them to mean anything.

If you go through something painful or an experience that evokes an emotional response but choose to block out the emotions, then you have not really gone through the experience. It's the act of actually processing the emotions that helps your mind learn and become better because of the experience, and if you miss this point, you will become a grown boy with scars that do not really mean anything. Since the experience has already hurt you, the least you can do is use it to draw on in the future; otherwise, it's all a waste. So let's do some practical work to get this truth to ring true in your life. Go through the challenge in the next section and do your best to follow it as closely as you can.

Challenge Your Walls

I know it's not easy to be vulnerable to someone else, especially as a guy surrounded by other men who tell you that it's a weakness to share your emotions and how you feel. If you have never done this, it would be a stretch to ask you to start by talking about your emotions right away. So instead, we are going to start slow and maybe remove one line of bricks from that wall.

First, you need a blank sheet of paper. You cannot use anything digital for this exercise, just paper and pen or pencil. Now I want you to think about one event, experience, or memory that you would never share with anyone because it makes you feel vulnerable. Whatever crosses your mind will do. Find a time and place when you can be alone and have about 10 minutes to spend on this challenge, and I want you to write about the event in as much detail as you can. You can even set an alarm and stop as soon as you hit the 10-minute mark.

As soon as you are done, take the paper and tear it up. You do not even have to keep the memory or share it with anyone else. Think of it this way: It will be like nothing ever happened after you tear up the paper, and the only person who will ever know what was written on it is you. It's a safe exercise. What you will notice, however, is that it feels so relieving to let out those emotions, even if just on paper in a few words.

I have dared so many people to do this, and the results have been humbling. I have met people whose first experience with vulnerability was through this exercise and got completely blown away by how it felt to let out some of that pent-up shame, anger, disappointment, resentment, and everything else in between. I want you to do this as soon as you can and see how it affects you as well.

After you have done this exercise, you can start to grow the parameters by doing it for longer, maybe half an hour of writing. You can sometimes decide to keep what you have written tucked away somewhere safe, and who knows, maybe you will even allow someone to read it at some point. This will be the start of your journey to learning how to be vulnerable, which is actually more important than learning about the truth itself. What is the value in a truth that cannot transform you?

It's amazing how you will begin to realize that being vulnerable has nothing to do with being weak. In fact, there is no greater act of courage than to voluntarily choose to become vulnerable. It's not easy at all to let out these emotions and learn to work through them, and it's not easy to allow yourself to be compassionate and empathetic. It's far easier to put the emotions away and rely on your physical strength to get you through everything. In the next chapter, we'll dig deeper into how you can show empathy and compassion as you begin to recognize others' emotions.

Third Truth: Emotional Strength in Men Is Exemplified Through Empathy and Compassion

In the last chapter, we started the conversation on empathy and compassion, two things that are often labeled as feminine traits but that you must possess in order to become a man. You cannot be a real man without learning to show empathy and compassion to yourself and the people around you. In fact, you cannot become anything without these important traits. Compassion and empathy are the doorway to understanding others and developing healthy relationships across the board. Obviously, this process starts with yourself, with understanding and showing compassion to yourself and affording yourself the grace and love it takes to care for your own needs and not let yourself degenerate with time.

In this chapter, we will go over what these two ideas really entail and help you start incorporating them into your character and conduct. I want you to see this chapter as a pit stop where you will change your mind and give yourself some tools that you will absolutely need if you are going to learn and apply the rest of the truths in this book. Because how you relate to people is important to who you are, you cannot become a better man if you do not take the time to learn how to understand and respond to the emotions of others.

Now let's look at empathy and see how it teaches you to speak and hear the language of feelings. If you are going to be effective at showing compassion, you will need to start with learning the basics of the language, and take it from me—feelings are a whole language all their own.

Cultivating Empathy

Simply put, empathy is the ability to understand how someone else feels. It's far more complicated than that, though, especially when you can hardly understand how you feel sometimes. This is actually a common mistake people make when it comes to empathy. Often, we think it's as easy as imagining we're in the same position as someone else, but this kind of empathy can come across as condescending and even do more harm than good.

True empathy does not assume but instead takes time to understand how the other sees the situation they are in and then listens before jumping to any conclusions. There is actually a funny line I learned from my grandfather. He would say, "I don't care if you walk a mile in my shoes. If you do not have my foot size, you will still never understand." This is very reflective of how most people see and approach empathy: pretending we are in the situation the other person is in and assuming that gives us a good idea of what they are going through.

In order to show empathy, you need to wear the person's shoes, walk around in them, and consider their size. The idea of understanding someone's shoe size brings a more personal perspective to the mix. You may not have to have a close bond with someone to walk in their shoes, but knowing their shoe size, so to speak, allows you to see things from their perspective while taking into account their life experiences and how those influence the way they see the world.

This will take some open-mindedness to achieve, and more than anything else, you will need to be compassionate enough to meet the other person where they are and be willing to listen and learn in order to connect with them. Regardless of what you think about who they are and how they live their life, you will have to give them what I like to call "respectful attention," which is listening respectfully and not giving an immediate answer when they are done. There are a few aspects of empathy that can help you understand and incorporate this truth into your life more effectively, and we are going to look at some of these now.

Active Listening

I remember when I was young and we had to wait around the radio for the news to come on. Either that, or we had to all gather around the TV so we could find out what was happening in the world. Because the internet was not as efficient as it is now, if you missed the news or did not hear what the news anchor said, then you would have to wait around until the next update to listen in again. Because of this, whenever the news was on, my father would have everyone quiet down, and he would listen as intently as he could to every word, knowing that if he missed what was said, he wouldn't be up-to-date until the next newscast.

That attention to detail is what you need to learn to have when you are listening to others. Imagine every word they say is very important and you do not want to miss a single sentence. The moment you give someone that level of attention, they will actually feel the atmosphere become safer for them to share how they feel.

In fact, your body language changes when you are listening to understand. You will turn your body toward the speaker and keep your eyes steady, almost as if you can see the words as they say them. But active listening goes beyond just listening attentively to what the other person is saying; it also encourages them to keep going and share their emotions.

Active listening is incorporating actions into your listening that tell the other person you are interested in what they are saying and want to hear more. It's in the way you nod, react with your face, position your body, and ask questions that probe the person to clarify and elaborate. That is what empathy is about—giving the other person space to tell you how they feel and what they are really going through. Unless they open up, you will not be able to understand how they really feel.

As you listen, try to validate the other person instead of questioning them. Keep in mind that questioning is different from asking questions. Asking questions is you genuinely trying to understand what is really going on, and questioning is you trying to invalidate what they are saying. When you are listening and trying to understand someone, validate how they feel even if you don't think they have justification for feeling that way.

I learned this from a former colleague of mine who was the ultimate overthinker. There was a time when the company was renewing the employee ID cards for everyone, and hers was not there with the first batch of cards that came back from human resources. Every morning until she finally got hers, she would come to my office to ask if I thought she was getting fired, had done something wrong, or some combination of the two.

I tried to explain to her that, just as HR had said, it was an error and they were working on it, but in her mind, there was something else going on. She always seemed to have these ideas that appeared to have no basis at all, and I eventually learned that the fear and anxiety were real for her. When her boss asked for her leave-day plans, she really thought it was because the boss hated her and wanted her to leave the company, even though every line manager was doing the same thing. But she didn't see it that way.

I had to learn to see the world the way she did before I could be a helpful friend to her. I had to realize that if I were in the same situation as her, I might not be as bothered, so I could definitely walk for a few miles in those shoes. However, I would not be able to go even half a mile in the same shoes with her feet as well. You need to learn to understand this concept. As I've mentioned, part of being a man is being the voice of reason and hope for those around you, and you will not be able to do this until you become genuinely empathetic toward others.

Situational Empathy and Diversity

Understanding others is also understanding that they are different from you. They have their own upbringing, their own culture, and their own way of seeing the world. We live in a world that has become more global yet more diverse at the same time. People from all over the world are now able to travel across the globe and even interact with other cultures without needing to travel at all. It's unbelievable how much technology has brought these borders down and given us access to ways of life that we did not know existed.

The big challenge, however, is that we are all different. While it's fun to work together and share our cultures, it might be harder to respect and understand another person's beliefs and culture, especially if they seem to clash with your own. You are not here to pick and choose what the next person believes, but you are here to show them your compassion, something you are best positioned to do when you are open-minded, accepting, and empathetic.

Being accepting of others' beliefs that are different from your own does not mean you have to adopt values that you do not believe in. No, you must be strong and stand for who and what you are without wavering. This is something we will actually go over in a later chapter as we look at how you can create and maintain good principles. But I digress. You should be able to show that you understand and accept another person but remain who you are, letting your light shine in its own way without trying to dim theirs.

The worst part is sometimes you find yourself in these situations before you have a chance to think about how to react to the people you are interacting with. If you do not have a sensitive heart and mind, you will be easily offended by people whose intentions were not to upset you, or you will end up causing offense when it was not your intention. That is why you should internalize these ideas by making them a part of who you are and a guide that is always there. It's not enough to have these truths as some collection of facts you just know. They need to guide and lead your conduct every day all the time.

So far, we have mostly been talking about understanding the people you work or go to school with and your friends. I know, however, that the main motivation and reason you probably want to change is because of the people who are dearest to your heart: your partner or your parents. These relationships are often too dynamic to build a mold around, but you can also apply these truths to them, especially the ideas of empathy and compassion. In the next section, we will talk about these closer, more intimate relationships and how you can use compassion to help make them stronger. This does not mean compassion is only for the people closest to you; no, you can use all of these truths in all areas of your life. That is what makes them so important—they will change your life no matter who you are or how you live.

Cultivating Compassion

Compassion is the next step after you use empathy. Imagine you are talking to someone or observing them, and through that, you begin to understand their pain, where they are in life, and how they need help, but you just walk away. What good will all your listening and attention have been? And I am certainly not saying you should always have an answer or good response to everything you observe to be a man. No, sometimes you will not have the answers. Sometimes you will have the wrong answers, and sometimes you will actually realize you are part of the problem.

Whether you have an answer or not, what matters is reacting to the world around you with compassion. As a man, you have probably heard "Keep your head up and your fists ready. Punch your way through life until you make it." Now, you might need to do some punching every now and then, but if all you do is punch, who will pick up the vulnerable people in our society when they trip and fall? Who will protect the weak when the punches start going their way? It doesn't have to be you every time, but it will always be men—those who recognize that there are problems weighing people down, who are aware of how broken the world can be and that sometimes they are responsible for breaking it, and those who are able to take responsibility for others, even when they don't have to.

Yes, you are right; that is how we defined a hero earlier, and it's how I want you to see yourself by the time you are halfway through this book. Showing compassion is a great way to get started on that. I would love to go over what compassion is, but

I have an even better idea: Let's go out and learn it practically. Now that we have gone over empathy, I know you are able to recognize someone in need when you see them. The next step is going out and spreading positivity to them however you can. In order to do this, we are going to look at two crucial elements to showing and practicing compassion—self-compassion and acts of kindness.

Self-Compassion

Charity begins at home. You will never be able to bring into the world anything you have failed to grow in your own life. My grandfather always used to say, "A man who farms yams sells yams." If you never planted yams, you will not be able to harvest and sell yams; and so it goes, if you do not learn to show compassion to yourself, you will never be able to show it to others. So let's talk about how you can show yourself compassion and what that looks like. For this section, you will need to have your journal handy as we will do a lot of introspection.

Jordan Peterson once said, "Treat yourself like someone you are responsible for helping" (2018). Imagine how that would change the way you look at yourself. We often treat ourselves very harshly, more harshly than we would treat the people around us and even our pets. In the same book, Peterson says

People are better at filling and properly administering prescription medication to their pets than to themselves. That's not good. Even from your pet's perspective, it's not good. Your pet (probably) loves you, and would be happier if you took your medication.

I have grown to understand why and how we treat ourselves the way we do. Think about it: You have been living with yourself all your life, and you are completely aware of all the evil that you have ever thought of doing and done. You know yourself, and you know about all your shortcomings and all the mistakes you have made. These often become a source of shame, guilt, and condemnation that distorts how you see yourself.

So the first thing I want you to do is forgive yourself. It's not easy to forgive yourself, especially when you are on a journey like this one. I believe you are pursuing these truths because you want to become better and be more responsible for your own actions. That is great, but it also creates a harsh self-judgment that might be difficult to escape. You will look at the ideal version of yourself—the one you are aspiring to be—and judge who you are now against that ideal. This puts you in a position of being disappointed in yourself every time you don't live up to that ideal. But you're human, and we all make mistakes. Having an ideal to aspire to doesn't mean you're not good enough if you fall short sometimes.

The best way to forgive yourself is to first change your standard for comparison to who you were yesterday rather than who you are going to be tomorrow. If you didn't care what you said last week but now you are more conscious about how your words can hurt people, then there is progress. The fact that your mind and heart are aware that what you did is wrong is enough to show that there has been a change within you. I want you to take this part seriously because it really carries so much weight and affects the rest of the project.

I want you to own this process and become the man you want to be. I want you to really see the change and really want the change to be evident in everything you do, but one thing is true: You need to forgive yourself first. You will learn what these truths are, but they will fail to mean anything to you because as long as you are holding your past mistakes against yourself, you will not be able to move on and become someone different.

In order to start the process of forgiving yourself, I want you to take some time to meditate and reflect on who you have been and who you think you want to be in the future. Really set this time aside and take your journal for the exercise. Write about your past and the present and then about who you want to transform into in as much detail as you can. When you are done, it's time for the magic step. I want you to imagine you are a judge presiding over your own life, ready to pass judgment on yourself.

Look at all the things you have done in the past, the things that you are not so proud of, and the things that bring you shame and guilt. Do you think they should go unpunished? If there is a chance that you can become a better man and make up for some of it, even if not directly but by bringing positivity into the world in your own way, would that not make up for the wrong you have done?

Now here is the judgment that you have to make: You can either condemn yourself and imprison yourself in guilt and shame for the rest of your life—something you might feel like you deserve—or you can forgive yourself with a promise to make things right and slowly grow into the opposite of who you have been. Which is the harder way out? It's harder to make changes to your thinking and behavior than to shackle yourself to the past without showing yourself any compassion or forgiveness.

It's hard to change. It's hard to learn what it means to be a real man and actually dedicate time to transforming your life so that you can become that person. That is your challenge—to drop all the guilt from your past because you will not be able to do any good unless you are a free man. You cannot keep yourself stuck in the past and still be a part of the change the future is looking for.

As soon as you forgive yourself, it's time for self-care, my favorite part of life. You have to practice showing love to yourself. You can love yourself first and see how it feels. You might even mess up doing it now and then, but that's okay. The best part is that all the self-love and compassion you have to give is stored in your mind, and you can bet there will come a time when it overflows. All the goodness you show yourself is like an investment into yourself for the future. You are slowly filling up your heart with goodness, and soon it will show. When you start to have empathy for others and genuinely feel like helping out every time you can, do not hold back; the fruits of your consistency are shining through.

I remember when I started taking good care of myself by being aware of what I ate, what I spent my time on, and how I invested my energy, and my life changed completely. The habits that I knew I needed, and even ones I didn't know I needed, started to develop and fill my life, and before I knew it, I was looking at myself differently. I was looking at myself with respect and love. When this happened, though, not everyone around me was happy or understood what was really happening.

I remember one of my friends telling me I was too self-indulgent and proud because of the way I would take care of myself and the environment around me. I thought about these words for so long and even started questioning if he was right and that I was just out there trying to gratify myself all this time.

I realized a few things during this time. The first was that I could not care about and show compassion to others if I stopped showing it to myself. It's amazing how strong the correlation is. The main reason I got back to working on myself and caring about myself was that I realized that if I did not, I could not give the same level of care, love, and attention to the people around me. I fell into this pit for a moment so that you would not have to.

You do not have to make the same mistakes I made. You are strong—stronger than you think, as a matter of fact. I did not know about these truths when I started this journey, but you have this great resource that will help you become everything you have ever wanted.

Acts of Kindness

I have a challenge for you for the next five days that I believe will help you learn to show compassion to the people around you. As you start to show compassion to yourself, you will naturally have a desire to extend the same goodness and care to the people around you, and that is where this challenge comes in. Your challenge is to show compassion intentionally five times in the next five days to different people. This can be fun and uplifting if you put your heart into it and really make it meaningful.

On the first day, your challenge is to compliment someone. It cannot be someone you compliment regularly already. Try to pick someone you have never given a compliment to and genuinely share one that you mean. I want you to go over to them and in the sincerest way, give them the compliment. You do not have to add anything on top of that, just a simple compliment given from the bottom of your heart. You are not restricted to what you can compliment as long as it is something genuine; you can compliment someone's clothing, the way they did something, or even something they do all the time that you have not acknowledged yet.

On the second day, I want you to double down on your compliments and give two different people compliments this time. The same rules from the first day still apply, so it has to be heartfelt and genuine, and the recipients have to be two different people who you don't normally compliment, and neither can be the same person you complimented the first day.

On the third day, as with the last two days, you are going to compliment three people, using the same rules as before. The addition to this day, however, is that you can show gratitude instead of giving a compliment. So you can either say thank you to all three people or you can split it whichever way you want between gratitude and compliments. Now, I know you are probably wondering why you have to compliment so many people for so long when there is so much more to kindness than the words you say. Well, firstly, the smallest act of kindness is as big as the biggest act of kindness as long as it's sincere. Your act of kindness, though small, will have a huge impact and brighten people's day just the same.

The other reason I want you to compliment someone every day is that it is a conditioning trick that will help you notice when the people around you do something well. Because you are actively looking for someone and something to compliment, your mind will be aware of all the people around you and all the good things they do. When you just go through life, you might miss all the good things that all the people around you are doing, but when you start intentionally looking for them, you will see all the great things that are happening all the time.

All of this will prepare you for days four and five when you are going to help someone out and get a gift for someone. On day four, I want you to think of how you can do something to make someone else's day better. A good place to start is at home, where there are so many chores to get done. You can pick one that was meant for someone else, giving them a chance to rest. This can also be done at school or work. In most cases, all you have to do is ask around and someone will take you up on your offer to help. Go to someone and simply say, "Is there anything I can do that would help make your day better?" I'm sure you will find at least one person with something you can help them with.

The last step is to use your finances on day five to show compassion to someone by buying them a gift. It can be anything, but it's even better if you buy them something they actually need. You have complete creative freedom for day five. You can spend as much as you want for anyone you want, and you can decide whether it will be a surprise or not. The reason this is the last action of the challenge is that money is the highest representation of our energy. That is to say, the things we use our money on are the things we value the most.

The idea with the challenge, of course, is not for you to just go through the motions and then go on with your life when you are done. I want this exercise to teach you to live a life of kindness, empathy, and compassion. Once you have done it for five days, what is to stop you from doing it for seven or eight days, or from turning it into a lifestyle? Everything we have gone over in this chapter creates a foundation for how we can live our lives so that we are cognizant of all the people around us and show them that they have value.

This is a process that starts with you and then moves on to the people around you and eventually has the power to spread to the entire world. From here, you can continue to strengthen your character, and there is no better way to do this than with the four pillars of resiliency, which we'll discuss in the next chapter.

Fourth Truth: True Masculinity Involves Prioritizing the Four Pillars of Resiliency

When I joined the Air Force, I had a very clear idea of what I thought it would do for me. I expected it would be like all the boot camps I had gone to as a teenager—fun and educational, but with the added benefit of actual authority and power. I could not wait to have the power and authority especially. One thing I had observed from people who had been in the military was how they could do nearly anything they put their minds to. It is almost as if they have a superpower that allows them to become whatever they want after they have gone through training with the Air Force.

To be honest, it is like that in a sense. There is a superpower that I got from being in the Air Force. It was not the power and authority that I thought it would be, but it was something else, something bigger: resiliency. According to the American Psychological Association, "Resilience is the process and outcome of successfully adapting to difficult or challenging life experiences, especially through mental, emotional, and behavioral flexibility and adjustment to external and internal demands" (*Resilience*, 2022). But I have a definition of my own; to me, resilience is the ability to push through a challenge or situation until the end regardless of the terrain and weather. I love this definition in particular because it's more than a metaphor for me. There was a time during training when I was going up a hill in the blistering cold rain with a load I did not know I could carry until I did it that day.

I remember thinking to myself that there was nothing I could not do. I clutched my bag, and with all my mind, whatever remained of my strength, the support of my colleagues pushing on next to me, and deep encouragement from my heart, I pushed until the end. These four things also happen to be the four pillars of resilience—four principles that can help you become unstoppable if you use them carefully. Now let's look at how you can apply these pillars in your life so you can see the growth that I have seen in mine.

The Four Pillars of Resiliency in the Air Force

When I mention the four resiliency pillars from the Air Force, most people are quick to dismiss it because it sound very specific to men of combat. This is actually not the case at all and could keep you from using a powerful tool to help you build your resilience. As Christenson, an Airman First Class says (2021):

In the U.S. Air Force, the four pillars of resilience are mental, physical, social, and spiritual wellbeing. These four pillars are the foundation of the Air Force Resilience Training Program used by Resilience Training Assistants and Master Resilience Trainers to help Airmen overcome challenges in their everyday lives.

The training is not meant only for the battlefield. It helps the airmen get over the hurdles that everyday life throws at them, which are the same challenges that you will face as a young man trying to find your place in the world. You know, you are a fighter in your own right. The challenges of life make everyone a soldier in their own way and force us to stand resiliently against the gunfire.

Now let's look at each of the four pillars individually and how they might help you become a better man for yourself, your family, and the society you live in. See this as your own mini boot camp: a chance to train and prepare yourself for the battles that are specific to you.

Mental

In the military, there is no better place to start than with your control base: the mind. All operations are monitored, controlled, and delegated from the base—this is where all the important decisions are made. Who you are is an extension of your mindset and your mental health, and it will be nearly impossible for you to live a strong and healthy life if your mental health is not stable. Everything hinges on it.

Recently, there has been a great surge in mental health issues, especially for young men. In fact, "one in seven young men aged between 16 and 24 experience depression or anxiety each year" (*Young Men*, n.d.). Mental health has to be addressed first because it is pivotal to the rest of the pillars—to the rest of the truths, actually. If your mind is not ready to support the life you are trying to live, then you will have a hard time attaining that life.

The main point of this book and of these truths is to help you create a mindset that will help you become a real man. You can see these truths as a code that will help reprogram your mind into being a real man. Following that analogy, imagine it as a step to arrange and plan your base of operations. You are making sure that the maps you are using to plan your attacks and defenses are accurate and that the intel and intentions you have will help you achieve your goals.

So how do you organize your mind to become resistant to all the information around you? How do you create a tenacious mental fortitude that will keep you going strong no matter what obstacles you meet along the way? There is one sure way to do this: feed your mind with the ideas that support your goals. You are already on that path as you read this book, so well done for that.

I want you to get even more intentional with what you expose your mind to. There are things you need to remove from your space and things that you need to add to it, and only you can figure out what those things are. Now I want you to get your journal and think through two questions that are key to controlling what you let into your mind.

The first question is what are some of the sources of information that make you nervous, anxious, and unsure of yourself? I want you to really think about how you feel about yourself after you get off social media or after you are done watching your favorite shows or even just listening to the news. This is the best way for you to figure out how the information you are consuming affects you. After you have thought about this, I want you to now think about some things you can stop doing to reduce the amount of media you expose yourself to that has a negative effect on you. Pick out something that you can stop, that you want to stop, and that you will make an effort to stop and give it a try.

On the other hand, all of those ideas you are trying to get out of your mind need to be replaced with new and better ideas that will reverse the effects. In your journal, write down the ideas that you think can combat the negative ones you are trying to get rid of. You become what you behold, and the more you interact with positive content, the better prepared your mind will be to support and grow your aspirations and dreams.

This is not a one-time exercise. Every now and then, you need to evaluate how you have been caring for your mind and what you have been feeding it. Ask yourself when you last read a good book or learned a new skill. Keep checking your progress as you go to make sure your mind is healthy.

Physical

Your body is the physical representation of who you are. While your mind decides on the things you do and the actions you take, it's your body that executes these actions. Your body is also what the people you interact with see. Because of this, it's important to make sure your physical presentation does justice to the mental frame we have created in the previous section.

Your body is an extension of your ideas and mental state; the correlation between the two is undeniable and will always shine through. If you are mentally healthy, it will show in the way you take care of your body, and vice versa. I want you to think of your body as having three different functions, and this will help you take care of it and monitor its health over time.

Your body is essentially there for storing and exerting energy, giving you a physical presentation, and allowing you to experience things. These are the three main ways in which we use our bodies, and making sure you are optimally positioned to do all of this will be a great advantage for you.

I want you to see your body as you do the battery inside your phone or laptop. It is what gives the device the energy it needs to do what has to be done. Your body is the source of energy for not only your physical activities, but it is also there to help with your cognitive ability and all the other functions that your body has. Just like a battery, your body can gain and lose power as you use it, and it can also be in good or poor health.

As a man, it is your responsibility to make sure you keep your body charged and full of energy. There are a number of ways you can ensure your body always has enough energy, including eating a healthy, well-rounded diet, getting regular exercise, and ensuring you get good sleep. These practices will help you make sure your body has the energy it needs to do what you need it to in order to make those dreams you have a reality. I know that you know all about proper diet, exercise, and all these other things that can help your body. The issue is hardly ever with knowledge but with intentionality and action. I want you to be intentional about taking care of your body and responsible for keeping it healthy and functioning optimally so that you can be as productive as possible.

Your body is also there for the aesthetic, the feel that people get when they see you. This is affected by how you dress and present yourself to other people. I am not saying you always have to be in a three-piece suit, but I am saying you should always communicate what you mean to communicate with your clothing. If you want to communicate that you are an eccentric artist who thinks outside the box, then convey that in how you dress. If you want to communicate that you are a trustworthy banker and people's investments will be safe with you, then dress in a way that demonstrates that. How you cut your hair, wear your clothes, clean your body, and smell are all signs of what you are about. It's like a shop front: If your appearance does not show people who you are and what you are about, no one will walk in—no one will want to talk to you. You are a brand, and you need to present that brand very well.

Last, and very important to me, is how your body and physical strength can serve to improve how you enjoy the world. You are created for adventure, and your body wants to enjoy and experience life as exciting as it comes. It's therefore your duty to make sure that you are healthy enough to experience and engage in those activities as much as you can. If you do not take good care of your body, you might not have the physical strength to experience the parts of the world that are there for you to enjoy.

Social

There is no denying that we are all social beings. Life is better when you are connected to the communities and groups that make it more interesting and worthwhile. I have seen so many young men choosing to live a reclusive lifestyle. The internet has made this an easier and far more expedient option over going out and meeting people physically. While there is nothing wrong with the community that the internet has built, and there is so much we can learn from it, we still need to be careful not to neglect a very important aspect of our inherent needs as humans.

Physical interaction is more important than any other type of connection or interaction you can have through any other medium. Humans have developed things like language and community much more effectively than any other species has been able to because we value social structures beyond the existence of the self. It's a very unique thing about human nature. If you take a man out of society, he will lose his mind—literally. It's the same as taking a fish out of water.

We grow and develop as individuals by interacting with others and using that information to frame the world around us and know how we can fit into our environment. In fact, we would not be able to create the schemas that make up our perception of the world today if it weren't for our social interactions with the people we grew up with, including family, friends, classmates, and community members. I could go on and on about how socializing is important to us as humans, but for now, I will give you a few hints on how you can positively increase your socialization as you prepare yourself for the growth that will come with embracing and living out these nine truths.

I want you to use your journal again—your new best friend—and record three things that you like doing. It can really be anything at all—work, hobbies, anything is fair game. Now I want you to think about how you can do these things with other people. Out of the three items on your list of interests, there should be at least one that can be done with other people physically, and if not, keep going down the list until you find something that you can physically do with another person.

You can use the internet to find groups and communities that share this interest, and then I want you to make the effort to show up for one of the events. When I did this exercise myself, I had chess, soccer, and food on my list. From this list, I decided to participate in physical chess tournaments and chess clubs rather than online games. I went to watch soccer games with friends and enjoyed cookouts whenever I was invited to one. This helped me get back into the social scene after burying myself in work and only connecting with others through social media.

Your situation might not look like mine. You might want to go to the gym, find people to jam with, start attending a local church, or join a book club. Whatever you do, make sure it helps you step out of your shell. Remember, you are not learning these truths for yourself; you are learning them so you can become a positive influence in the lives of the people you love and your community. If you are not a physical presence in the lives of these very people you are trying to reach, you will have a very hard time becoming the leader you want to be.

Spiritual

I have had so many conversations with young men who are struggling and trying to get their lives in order. I often ask them about the state of their spirituality, and they will immediately reply with "I don't believe in any of that" or some variation of that remark. I think we have done a horrible job as a society of defining what spirituality is and why it is important for everyone to explore and nurture their individual spirituality.

Spirituality is the practice of finding meaning beyond ourselves and our current circumstances. It's the act of believing that there is more to who we are than what we perceive in our lives currently, and if we seek the truth and true value of our lives, we can find it apart from ourselves. It's not about a church or denomination or conjuring spirits to consult about your life and future.

While some of those things might have some value and a place in some people's spirituality, I will not focus on any of them. Instead, I will focus on how you can become more aware of yourself so that you can become more aware of the world you exist in and your purpose within it. Now let's go back to the problem and see how this idea can help us find a solution. The issue is that you are trying to orient yourself in the world in a way that sets you on the path to finding meaning and sharing that meaning with everyone else.

The meaning has to be greater than you, otherwise, your limit would be who you are today. So it has to be a force beyond yourself—an ideal that presents itself as supreme to what you currently know and experience. It cannot be drawn from within, and it cannot be framed within your understanding. Let's be candid: You have known yourself all your life, and you probably know by now that you need the support of something bigger than yourself to get you to reach your goals and ambitions.

So now I want you to ask yourself what your heart is hoping for and what the anchor for that hope is. What are your ambitions and what truths are they trying to satisfy? Your hopes and ambitions should be bigger than you and bigger than your current reality. Create an elaborate picture in your mind of the ideal version of yourself and pair that with what the ideal version of your life would be like. In fact, write these down in your journal so you have a record of your ultimate ideal.

This ultimate version of yourself may not be something you will likely ever attain, but it's something you need to have as a guide and as a point of reference that you look up to and compare yourself to. This is why religions have these descriptions of God, Jesus, and other figures that call us to live up to that standard.

Having an ideal version of yourself is one thing, but you will also need to intentionally orient your mind and heart to pursue that ideal every moment of your life. Having a good spiritual life is living life in constant pursuit of what is good and in a position of working toward embodying that ideal. I encourage you to find your own way of defining what your ideal is and how you want to prepare your heart to pursue it. Do not leave this to chance to get ahead.

Now that you have learned the truth about resilience and how to build it, who or what can stop you now? Other than yourself of course. As I have said, you are the only person who can topple these pillars if you choose to. You are the greatest and maybe only threat to your success. If you fail to properly coordinate your mind, strength, social engagement, and spirituality to make yourself stronger and invincible, then you will fail to reach goals that you otherwise would.

Do not take for granted the power you can channel through your own mind and spirit, the way your body can store and use that power, and how your community can lift you up as you reach for your goals. Nothing is impossible. You can become the man you are meant to be and share that strength with the people around you. Resilience is a great superpower to have. Now let's look at how you can fortify it by learning to continuously grow and bounce back when you fall.

Fifth Truth: Being a Man Lies in Your Capacity to Grow as an Individual and Bounce Back Stronger From Life's Setbacks

How many times have you failed in the past week, month, or even year? How many times have you tried something only to realize you were really bad at it? More often than you would be comfortable admitting, I imagine. But so what? This is everyone's tale. We are all failing at something every day, especially the ones who end up succeeding. The problem is that we see our own failures, but we do not see the failures of the people around us, and that creates this false perception that we are the only ones failing. But trust me, everyone fails, every single person.

Now the truth I want you to understand here has two parts. First, I need you to know that being a man is about bouncing back when you fail, and beyond that, it's about pursuing growth. You need to understand that you can come back when you feel like it's impossible. It's only then that you can grow and become better than you were when you failed. Imagine it this way: You only fail when to try to do something better than you were doing it before.

I like to use the example of mathematics. Math is not equally hard from when you start school to when you are in college. While it will feel hard at every stage, it is not, and it actually gets progressively harder. This means that while you may still fail and struggle with math all the way to your freshman year, you will still be far better at it when you get there than you were when you first started. There will always be another concept to learn that will not be as easy as what you already know, but that doesn't mean you can't learn it, too, and move on to the next new concept, continuing to get better than you were before.

That being said, life will always have challenges for you, and you will fail every now and then, but that does not mean that you have not gotten any better or that you are not growing. In fact, if you stop failing at anything, that might be an actual cause for concern. You might have gotten stuck in a fixed mindset and strangled your own growth instead of letting it thrive.

Embracing Failure

The first thing you need to do is get rid of your fear of failure. If you are afraid you will fail, then you are more likely to fail, but you will also be more likely to run from everything that could lead to your failure. Think back five years, or even more if you can. What was your biggest failure back then? Do you think anyone is still talking about that failure or even remembers it? I can assure you that no one is still talking about it and even if they remember it, no one cares.

It's the truth: No one cares about what you tried to do and failed. They do not care that you have tried to start a business seven times and failed or that you have been learning to code for months and it's still challenging for you. No one is famous for failing unless they make it in the end. If all you do is fail, no one will think about it or talk about it, so there is nothing to be afraid of. I wish this assurance itself could stop you from fearing failure, but I know it does not really work that way. So we are going to look at some ways you can overcome the fear of failure, and we'll also talk about how you can change your mindset to help you keep going when you feel like a failure.

Not All Failure Is Failure

The first thing you can do to get from the point of fearing failure to learning from it is what I call failure analysis. For this, you will need your journal again and a safe, quiet space where your thoughts can flow in peace. Once you have these in place, I want you to start off by thinking about a time you think you failed and why you think that is before you even write anything. It's so common for people to think they have failed when they actually have not.

I have spoken to students who got a 90% on an exam and still see it as a failure. I have known people who tried to start a business and grow it to a million-dollar enterprise within a year and felt like failures when it did not happen. There is a difference between failing to reach a goal and failing to meet your potential. If what you failed to do is something no one can do or that you never would have been able to do given your ability and capacity, then you have not really failed. If you try to run up Mount Everest in half an hour, you will not be successful, but you cannot count that as a failure. That example seems obvious, but this is true at so many levels, even down to small things you might blame yourself for but that you could not have done any differently.

Narrow Down and Define Your Failure

After you eliminate all the things that you thought were failures but that are not, it's time to do some more introspection and journaling. Write down all the major failures you have had in the past few months in your journal. Now rank them so that the most important is at the top and then pick out the top three failures. These are the ones we are going to be using for the exercise.

You are going to look at each of these three things and use them to shift the focus of your mind from condemnation and shame to learning and growth. The first question I want you to answer in your journal is how could you have done things differently? Thinking about this question is not the same as mindlessly overthinking about the past where you reminisce and replay scenarios in your head. Instead, this is about you genuinely wondering and looking for ways for how you can do things differently the next time you try to do something new.

Explain to yourself all the parts of the attempt you failed at and all the things you could have done differently. One possible outcome of this exercise is realizing that there truly was nothing you did wrong and nothing you could have done differently; it may turn out to be another case where you thought you failed but really didn't. However, if this is not the case, write down what exactly you failed at and try to be detailed about specific areas that are measurable.

If you start a business and it does not go well, that does not mean you failed in every way; maybe your marketing was weak and you never got clients but everything else was great. Maybe you had a bad product and need to decide how to improve that, or maybe the whole thing was bad—which is hardly ever the case. Thinking about where specifically you failed makes what you need to work on clearer and more obvious. If you say, "I tried a business and failed," there is nowhere to go from there and nothing you can take steps to improve on. On the other hand, saying "I failed because of my marketing strategies" means you know what you have to do before you dust yourself off and try again.

This part of the process can be hard since you will have to revisit the memory of the failure and think about it all over again. But that is okay. You may find that knowing how and what exactly you failed at will actually make the failure feel and look smaller. Knowing you failed at only one component of a project is different from assuming you failed at the whole thing, and you need that distinction.

Plan for Your Improvement

Okay, so now not only do you know that you failed, but you also know what you failed at and why. You know the exact problem, and you know what skills you need to gain to make sure it does not happen again. It's time to make a plan for the learning curve. Most people say we learn from our experiences, and while that carries a lot of truth, it's also not always the full truth.

You not only learn from your experiences but also from the actions you take after a failure. Think of it this way: Each experience shows where you fall short and need to improve, but that does not necessarily translate to learning. You need to then take the pain point highlighted from your experience and do something about it. If you fail to make the team because you do not run fast enough, you have learned that you need to start training so you can run faster, but that information is useless if you do not take steps to get yourself to be a faster runner.

So for each of the three areas you highlighted in the previous section, I want you to take some time and think about what you can do, what you would like to do, and what you are able to do to cover the areas of inadequacy. You might need to start by reading some material, practicing, consulting, or something else. It has to be something that you would actually do and have the will, time, and resources to do. After you have made your improvement plan, put it everywhere. Make it a part of your development goals and a part of your calendar, and you can even put sticky notes on your fridge or bathroom mirror if you would like.

This is how you fight failure and grow your resilience. You cannot bounce back unless you take the time and put in effort to make it happen. You cannot just read these truths; you have to do every exercise and take every moment of reflection seriously because the point of all of it is to genuinely bring you transformation and growth. Now let's look at the idea of growth and go over how you can use your mind to create and sustain growth in your life.

Building a Growth Mindset

The idea of a growth mindset was made popular by Carol Dweck in her book, *Mindset: The New Psychology of Success* (2006). I have read this book so many times because, while the idea is somewhat straightforward, it's one that is easy to miss. The idea is that there are two types of mindsets: One is the growth mindset, and the other is the fixed mindset. The difference between the two is not whether or not you are successful in life but whether or not you believe you have the ability to grow and change as an individual.

A growth mindset is defined by the belief that you have the ability to learn new things, and this mindset will always help keep you going by focusing on what you did right and what you can do differently to get better results next time. When you have developed a growth mindset, you will ask questions like *How can I do this better? Where can I improve? Who should I reach out to for help?* The idea is that if something does not go the way you wanted it to, you need to try something different next time to get the results you want.

On the other hand, a fixed mindset has you believe that you are not capable of learning anything new or gaining any new skills, and it will look at all failure as a sign to quit. When you have a fixed mindset and you fail at something, you are likely to just give up and move on to something else. There is an insistence that all talent for something comes from birth, and if you can't do something, it means you were never meant to do it in the first place. This has been debunked a number of times, and one example is with chess. It was proven that teaching a child to play chess—or any musical instrument actually—would make it more likely that the child would become a prodigy. As you can see, this directly contradicts the laws of the fixed mindset and suggests that we are not born great, but instead, we are all born with the ability to be great.

If you work hard, you can become great. You have the potential within you, and if you choose to let it out, you will become the man you are supposed to be. It can be hard to really become the person you should be when you are not intentionally trying to improve yourself. There is no easy path that will make you feel like you are good enough, and you need to find what your gifts are. If you happen to find your gifts, it might still be hard for you to grow because even your passions need hard work and dedication before you can see the results you are looking for.

One thing that I can guarantee you is that there is a very serious connection between hard work and success. There is no getting around this. Your success is a reflection of how hard and diligently you are working. This is like a scale that the universe has put into place, and it really helps the world function. I mean, think about it: We would never want to be part of a society that believes you should get whatever you want without working for it.

Praising and giving due honor to those who have worked really hard will help improve the quality of life for the whole community and promote growth like never before. This is also groundwork for the truth we are going to discuss next, which is honoring your word and seeing your promises through.

Sixth Truth: A Man's Strength Lies in His Ability to Honor His Word and See His Promises Through

One thing that you always have control over is your word. You control what you say, when you say it, and how you say it. Even if you do not have any wealth, power, or influence, you still have your word, and that is more than enough to help you build character. A real man keeps his word and respects his own word above anything else.

Your words are an extension of who you are; that is to say, your words are you. When your words are false, you become a fraud, and when you do not follow through on your word, you become a liar, and when your word is deceptive, you are seen as a deceiver. Your reputation hangs on the very words you say. In this chapter, we are going to talk about honor and integrity and how your word can help you build your character and reputation in the community you live in.

Taking Ownership

The first thing you need to learn so you can become the master of your own character is to own up to everything you say. You see, speech is a tool that is often misused. So many people say what they think they should to get their way. People use speech to manipulate and cheat others all the time, but you do not want that to ever be you.

The ability to properly use speech even when most people are misusing it and when it is so easy to misuse will help you develop a very strong moral campus. If you see an opportunity to lie or make grand statements to make yourself look better and don't fall into the trap of doing so, that shows great strength and self-control. That alone puts you ahead in the race of life as it establishes you as a strong and principled man.

Even when your word does not have the impact you thought it would, you still have the obligation as a man to stand by it and own up to your mistakes. One thing I learned early is that you would rather back up your word with an apology than with an excuse. Giving an excuse means you're acknowledging that responsibility needs to be taken, but you'll pass it off to the next person the first chance you get; giving an apology means you realize a mistake was made and you are taking responsibility for it in an attempt to make things right.

A man who accepts responsibility for his failures and mistakes is more likely to be trusted the next time because, despite the mistake, his taking accountability shows he is willing to learn and do better. In fact, when you have failed to live up to your word or realize that you have failed to do something in general, give an apology with a promise. If you failed a test and are apologizing to your parents, don't just say, "I'm sorry I failed my test." Add a reason for the failure and tell them what you are going to do to make things right and do better on the next test. So you might apologize first, explain what happened that made you fail, and promise to spend more time studying next time. That is what a real man does—he handles his failures himself and does not look for someone to lay all of the blame on. And this is what I am inviting you to become.

You have to be aware that everything you do will have an impact on the next person whether you intend for it to or not. When you make your apology or accept the blame for failing to keep your word, you should be aware of the people who were hurt, disappointed, and misled because you failed to keep your word. This should not come from a place of blame and condemnation but rather a place of responsibility. You should do this because it shows that you understand that what you do has a big impact on others.

Honoring Commitments

As a man, the people around you need to know that they can count on you whenever you make a promise. This is how you start to build trust and reliability within your community. You may not be giving your word to the community at large right away, but you can start by doing this with your friends and family, and this will help you practice these actions and apply them in every situation you find yourself in now and in the future.

As you grow and start to get into professional relationships, you will see how important trust is. Your work can be one part of an entire project that depends on you to finish your part in order to be completed. When you are in these situations, you will realize how important it is that people are able to trust your word and plan around it. However, you cannot suddenly develop this when you first find yourself in these situations; you need to work on developing that integrity now, as you are learning how to become the man you will be then.

Look into your future and see the type of person you want to be, and allow that to guide how you work to incorporate these truths into your life. I say this to so many young men who are trying to grow into respectable and honorable men who can genuinely lead and impact the world. It's not about what you are going to become then, it's about what you are now. Who you are now will simply amplify as you grow up, so whatever you want to become, it's best to start working toward that now.

Then there is the other angle you need to look at: You should not become a slave to your word. When you make a promise, it's important that you wholeheartedly mean it and want to follow through on it. However, things can change, and there might come a time when you can no longer fulfill a promise you have made, and this is okay. You do not have to tie yourself to something you said when it no longer fits with what you really need to do in the moment and what you have planned moving forward.

What you need to do, however, if you are ever in a position where you are no longer able to fulfill your word is communicate. You should go to the person you made the promise to and explain why you are unable to keep the promise any longer. Most people will be grateful when you come to them and are honest about how and why you can no longer uphold your promise. This shows integrity on your part and allows them to make any necessary changes to their plans.

Communication is such a powerful tool, and you can use it to your advantage whenever you need to. Clearly and honestly communicate your position every time you have to. If you have the intention to do something, communicate it out loud. When you fail to deliver on a promise that you have made, let the people you made the promise to know and give them an explanation as to why.

Overall, you need to learn to honor your word. Other people will only honor and respect what you say to the extent that you do so yourself. You will notice that as you start to honor your word more, you will become more intentional with what you say. The more you care about what you say, the more careful you will be about what you say. Thus, honoring what you say is not only about keeping your word once you make it, but it is also about being mindful of every word you speak all the time.

Personal Accountability

What comes to your mind when you hear the word "accountability"? Do you think of someone standing over your shoulder with a checklist keeping track of everything you do and disciplining you when you do something wrong? I know this is a common view of accountability among young men these days. While this can be one component of accountability, it's not even half of the story. Accountability is about acknowledging your responsibility, recognizing your growth, and measuring how far you have come.

I want you to think of accountability as simply accounting, or to simplify further, counting. It's when you set up a system to "count," or keep track of, what you have done right and what you have done wrong so you can take responsibility for any mistakes and figure out ways to do better next time. That's the basis of it really—to figure out where you might be going wrong and start planning your return to the path you should be on.

Don't forget, though, that accountability is also about counting the things you do right. It's not all about looking at what went wrong and how you played a part in it because you need to have a record of what you are doing right and take time to celebrate those moments. I want you to flip the meaning of accountability in your mind right now from the negative aspects of punishment and discipline to the positive view of growth and celebration. Once you have done this, it will be very easy for you to become accountable to others and live a transparent and honest life.

You cannot be accountable to everyone about everything, so one of the things you will have to do is find accountability partners for different parts of your life. In all of this, you are your biggest accountability partner. You will have to hold yourself accountable for how you spend your money, time, and energy. You spend more time with yourself than anyone else, so if anyone can really evaluate your behavior, it's you. Plus, let's be honest, you can sometimes deceive everyone else, but you cannot deceive yourself.

After you have learned to be accountable to yourself, you need to then become accountable to your partner, close friends, and family. These are all people whose lives are directly affected by how your life goes, so you owe them some level of transparency about how things are going for you. You are not an island, and thank God for that. You are meant to have a community of support around you, and this is why you need to be accountable to all these people.

The Role of Integrity

In my view, integrity is basically aligning your actions with your values and principles. What you say you believe should be what guides what you do and how you do it. Therefore, the first thing you need to do as you work to develop a sense of integrity is to decide what principles and values guide your life. It's important to have these ideas clearly defined in your mind if they are going to help you to become a successful and impactful man.

You might not have noticed, but part of the goal of each of these truths is to help you come up with a value structure that is ethical, effective, and impactful. If you incorporate the truths in this book into your choices, actions, and daily life, you will already have a good basis for your value system, and all you will have to do is add the elements that relate directly to your life so that the value system works for you.

As I have said from the beginning, you are not meant to just read through and enjoy this book—though I hope you do. Rather, the idea is for you to internalize everything and mix it all up with your own ambitions and goals to define the truths that will help you create the best and most authentic version of your life possible. The more you apply these truths, the more you will see them affect your life and shape your future.

Looking at the truths we have covered already, you can see that a good value system should be grounded in compassion, proper use of power, resilience, emotional intelligence, and empathy. Now I want you to grab your journal again and write down how you will incorporate these things into your life.

I want you to look at your hobbies, interests, and the social environment you are in and seriously think about how these values can be implemented in your life.

Once you figure out how to use these truths, that becomes your standard for integrity. You will be living to meet and surpass that standard, knowing it's a limit that allows you to grow as an individual as you also help support and improve the lives of the people around you. You want to make sure you're always fulfilling both sides of the obligations in your life—those to yourself and those to your family, friends, and community. You do not want to focus on yourself so much that you become useless to the world around you, but you also do not want to be so focused on changing the world that you forget to take care of yourself.

Ethical Decision-Making

Once you have your standard for ethical behavior, it's time to set it as the filter you use when you are making decisions. Every decision you make has to be seen through the lens of your structure of values. This means that before you commit to doing anything, you need to ask yourself if it will add to your life and if it will help you give more to the world around you. If you can't say yes to either of these things, then you may need to re-evaluate your decision.

You should know that it will not always be easy to make decisions, even when you have a clear value system and clear principles. There are so many things that you will have to consider in every individual situation that will require you to think carefully and critically. There are things like ethical dilemmas that can arise in the moment, and you will have to train yourself to integrate what you know into a creative solution when that happens.

Lucky for you, we live in a world where there are many situations in which you can learn how to navigate ethical issues confidently and reach meaningful solutions. We live in a time when we are trying to resolve issues like gender inequality, sexual identity differences, and race, among many others. While I cannot tell you how to handle each of these situations, if you use the framework that is provided by these truths, then you will have a good basis for navigating each of these thoughtfully and empathetically.

In addition to being certain and holding on to your principles and values, I also advise you to look at the situation from the other person's or group's perspective. We are all so different and see the world and life so differently, and because of this, you should always be open to seeing the world how others do. Gaining perspective and understanding how the other person feels before you go ahead and make a decision is an important part of empathy.

I therefore invite you to keep an open mind as you interact with others and listen before you make an attempt to help. I know so many people make the mistake of diving in to give their opinion before they fully hear the other person because they believe they have the answer or know better. Well, you may know more than most people, but as I always say, you should assume the person you are talking to knows something that you do not, and maybe you will learn something new.

In addition to listening to the other person before jumping in with a response, you can also ask for advice or guidance from mentors, teachers, leaders, and anyone else you know who holds the same values as you but has more wisdom. It's a great virtue to be able to humble yourself to ask for assistance and advice from people who know better than you. And yes, there is always going to be someone who knows better than you.

The best way to get advice is to make sure you always have the three levels of mentorship in place in your life. First, you want to have people who look up to you as their mentor. If you do not have anyone in this category, don't worry; you can always start by being a mentor to yourself. After this, you should have a friend that you are learning with. This is someone who is at the same level as you who you can bounce ideas off of and who has the same goals and values as you do.

A friend is great to have when it comes to decision-making because they will help you think from the ground up and really apply yourself since you're both looking for the answer. If you have the right group of people around you, you will be able to get advice for nearly everything from one or two of your friends just as you will be able to give them assistance on one or two topics as well.

Lastly, you should have a mentor who leads you as you grow to become the man you want to be. This book acts as a mentor, explaining the truths that you might not hear all the time and helping you to become a better person than you were yesterday. Unfortunately, it cannot answer your questions in real time or listen to you share your brilliant ideas, so you will still need to have a mentor in addition. You need to find someone you trust and who shares your principles with more experience than you so they have somewhere to draw the wisdom from.

Once you have a mentor, create an honest and candid relationship with them. You don't have to give them the final say over your life—you are still accountable and responsible for your own actions. All that mentor is there to do is guide you as you navigate through life.

How does it feel knowing that you have the power to control your character and that you can shape it through your words and actions? If I am being honest, I found it quite intimidating when I first figured it out. It can be overwhelming knowing that your life is not in the hands of anyone other than you and that you will bear the responsibility for every word you say and every action you take.

However, once I started to realize that, I also realized that I had the ability to become whoever and whatever I wanted to be and that I had control over how successful and impactful I would become, and I started warming up to this idea. I want you to think of all the good you want to see in your life, in the lives of your loved ones, and in the world in general. You have a say in whether that will ever become reality. That is how powerful your decisions are. Therefore, I want you to seriously think about what this truth means to you and how you are going to integrate it into your life.

You are a man of integrity, honor, and wisdom; do not let that be taken away from you. It is these values that will help you maintain grit, perseverance, and resilience in the face of adversity. In the next chapter, we will look at how all the truths we have gone over so far come together to help you develop and maintain a strong and unbeatable character that will lead you to become the person you really want to become.

Seventh Truth: Strong Men Prioritize Their Ability to Maintain Grit, Resilience, and Perseverance in the Face of Adversity

The world will always have some difficulty to throw your way. I have found that everyone is always facing something all the time; maybe it's sickness, financial difficulty, or relationship problems, but we all have our share of obstacles and tragedy and therefore need to learn to function in a world that is as flawed and challenging as the one we live in.

I remember a story I heard from my mother once that has helped me understand how to remain resilient regardless of what is happening around me. As the story goes, there was a man who went to see a doctor because it seemed as if his life was full of difficulty, and no matter how hard he tried to get around that, he would always find himself right back in the same place again. After a few conversations with a therapist, the man left and looked for a new therapist as he did not agree with what the first therapist had been saying.

He found another therapist, and his wife tagged along to his sessions just in case she could be any help. After a few weeks, they left this therapist as well and switched to another one. This happened a few more times until the wife thought she would step in and stop all the madness that was now costing them a fortune. She told him he could choose one more therapist, but that would be the last one. If he did not like them, he could stop seeing someone altogether, but there was no space to choose another, and this was his last chance to get help from someone.

On the first day the man went in for therapy, he told the therapist how his world felt empty, difficult, and full of pain. He talked about how no matter what he did and how he did it, there was always something at the end of the sprint to break him and bring him down again. Just before the doctor could respond, the man stepped in and warned the therapist sternly, "You are my last chance to see a therapist and get help. So please do not ruin this for me. Do not tell me about how the people around me are inconsiderate, how the government and all the other institutions are not working in my favor. Do not tell me it's my parents, my colleagues, or my boss who are causing my stress. I have heard that narrative over and over again from many different therapists, and it's the reason I have been moving. You see, if you tell me everyone around me is the problem and not me, well, that means I am trapped and cursed to live this slow, mundane, painful life for the rest of my life. I cannot do anything to change my parents, the government, or anything else other than myself. So please, tell me how all of this is my fault and how I can change myself to make my life better."

After the long plea, both the therapist and the man's wife were left speechless, trying to make sense of what the man had just said. When I heard this, I also just sat there trying to make sense of the story. Eventually, my mother explained that this man had solved the main problem in his life, and it's a problem that most people have but instead of working to fix it, they tend to nurture it and let it get worse.

If the rest of the world is at fault for your tragedies, then there is nothing you can do to end them and live a better life. Even worse, you would then be bound to spend the rest of your life stuck in the delusion that the world owes you peace and comfort when it really does not. This can make you entitled and lead you to chase a path of dominance and greed instead of seeking continuous improvement and growth. You are already on the path of growth, though, and you will only get better at it.

Grit and Perseverance

Grit is the ability to keep chasing all your ambitions passionately even when the challenges you meet along the way seem insurmountable. As a man, you need to have a passion for your ambitions so strong that you are able to fight through anything to reach for them. You need to believe strongly enough in the goals you have set for yourself to overcome any obstacle to see them become reality. If you do not have anything meaningful to live and fight for, then you will die for anything.

You first need to understand that it is all up to you. No matter how hard the world around you gets, you cannot let that determine how your life goes. You are in control, and if you blame the state of your life on the actions and mistakes of others, you will only sink further into despair and helplessness. So I invite you to learn to accept all responsibility for your life and then find the ambition and motivation within yourself to fight for your dreams with all your heart.

Let's talk about goals for a moment. You need to have goals if you are going to be effective and efficient in life. I want you to think of yourself as a tool, and the more specific your mission is, the more useful a tool you will be. Imagine you go to a blacksmith and request that they make you a tool that can be used for cutting down trees, farming, stabbing, being thrown like a javelin, and protecting you like a shield. While they can create something that brings together all of these functions, this tool will probably not be very good at any of them. It will have to give up so much and so many elements will be compromised just so it can do all these things that it will be good for nothing in the end.

In the same way, you also need to be very specific about your goals so that you can focus on becoming the best tool to achieve your purpose. When you have a specific goal that you are working toward with all your heart and strength, you will be more likely to use your resilience and grit in the process. You will value this journey more because it's all you have and you therefore need to protect it. If you do not have a goal that you are willing to give your energy to in this way, it will be really easy for trouble to lead you astray.

Adaptability and Flexibility

We cannot talk about being resilient and having grit without talking about adaptability and flexibility. It's not enough to keep pushing when things get hard; sometimes it's better to change paths and leave the obstacle where it is. In most cases, you just need to be creative and come up with new solutions to your problem instead of taking action without planning what you will do.

Let's talk about how you can learn to improve your adaptability skills and use them to keep going even in this diverse and ever-changing world. With all the advances in technology and how the social landscape has been evolving over the past few years, you really need to be flexible now more than ever. You might be focused on personal development, but if you do not learn the nuances of the social landscape, then that might not count for much. You are like a vine in the jungle: As you grow, you need to wrap yourself around society and grow along with it.

Change is a natural part of life. In fact, change is the only constant that is guaranteed in life. Nothing will ever remain the same, so you need to have a mindset that is accepting of change and that is capable of dealing with it properly when it comes around. When the rug gets pulled out from under you, do not allow yourself to be taken by surprise and lose your balance. Instead, find something to hold on to that will keep you grounded and focused. Find new ways to keep going no matter what happens. I cannot give you individual solutions to the problems that you will face because I can't predict what challenges will arise in your life. What I can do is teach you to develop a creative, flexible, and adaptive mind.

In order to have the right mindset for this, you must start training yourself now. You do not need to wait for the big changes or tragedies to hit to start practicing adaptability. There are already so many changes around you that you can look at and learn from. I want you to grab your journal and think about this question: How can you change the way you are currently doing things so you can become more efficient? Your efficiency can be measured by how you use your time, resources, and energy, so think about these things first as you try to figure out how you can adapt to be as efficient as possible.

First, think about how you can change the way you do things currently and how you can get more done in the amount of time you have. This is not always easy, but once you consider how technology has developed over the past few years, you might start to get some answers. To build on that, here's another question for you to think about: How can you use less of your energy and still get the same results or better from your life? When you look at the things that you have to do, you can then evaluate and see if there are some things that technology has made easier or that you do not have to do anymore.

When you do this, your mind will start to bring to your attention things that you can do to improve your life. As you meet new challenges along the way, your mind will stay within that framework and always look for the most efficient way to solve the problem. You need to constantly evaluate whether you are using your resources and energy as well as you can. Challenge the methods that you are using right now and try to improve them where possible. That is what you are—the fighter who always wins in the end.

The Power of Positive Thinking

Whenever things stop going my way or according to the plan, I tell myself it's time to find a new way to get this done. I always challenge myself to focus on what I can still do despite the hurdles in front of me, and I have realized that it has saved my mental health and helped me reach goals that once seemed impossible. I like to look at every journey like going through a maze; sometimes you will feel like you are going in the right direction, but before you know it, you hit a dead end. When you hit a dead end, you just need to turn around and try to find another route until you eventually make it out. Sometimes you will go right, sometimes left, and sometimes you will even feel like you are going backward, but that's okay. The important thing is that you keep going and do not stop no matter what.

As a young man trying to find meaning, I dare you to carry the same mentality as well. I dare you to become so focused on finding a way out that you do not spend time complaining that you're stuck at a dead end. There will always be something to complain about, so if you start now, you will never stop.

Something that is really profound about the maze analogy is that if you are ever going to get out, you need to remember where the roadblocks are. As you go through the maze, you do not just keep randomly moving in any direction. No, you have to remember which paths have led you nowhere so that you can avoid going down them again. This is how you need to navigate your life as well. If you do something that does not work, remember that and avoid going down that same path again.

My father always used to say being stupid is doing the same thing over and over and expecting different results. If you keep trying to do the same thing—going down the same path when it is clearly not working for you—then your demise will be in the maze and you will never find a way out. One way to keep from getting stuck in the maze is to journal your attempts as much as you can. Keep a record of what you are doing, what is working, and what is not, then record what your next step will be and how you modified it based on what you've learned.

Continuous Learning and Curiosity

There is always something new for you to learn and add to your bag of skills. Learning is how you integrated yourself into the world when you were still a child. You were curious, and that helped you try to learn everything you could. That curiosity has helped you create a good understanding of your environment.

As we grow, our curiosity starts to fade away, and we lose the wonder of our younger years. It's on you to rekindle that curiosity and thirst for knowledge in your life. If you do this well, it will lead you to many amazing discoveries and allow you more room to improve yourself. Make sure you are learning something new all the time. It might be learning a whole new skill or reading a book that touches on something you are interested in. As long as you are expanding your knowledge, you are on the right path.

You can learn a new sport, pick up a new hobby, or do anything that will keep a different part of your mind active and bring you joy. In my own quest to keep my mind engaged, I have learned to play chess and the acoustic guitar, and now I am planning to start learning tennis. The mind loves to have something new to do so it can keep expanding. Another truth, however, is that you are only as resilient as the people around you. So while you have now prepared yourself for the adversities that lie ahead, you need to surround yourself with people who will help you stay on the path of resilience. Let's move on to the next chapter and see how the company you keep will influence the type of person you become.

Eighth Truth: True Masculinity Includes Recognizing the Value of Surrounding Yourself With People Who Align With Your Goals and Values

Imagine you are in an accident that leaves you unconscious and in a coma for a long time. After a few weeks of examinations and tests, the doctor concludes that you are going to be okay, but it will be three years until you wake up again. The procedure they are going to use will take that long to work, but it's guaranteed that you will wake up and be able to resume living your normal life.

In the meantime, your friends are given the chance to make all the major life decisions you would have made had you been awake the whole time. When you wake up, you will not have to catch up with anything, and it will be like you were there and made all the decisions you needed to. Now I want you to really think about this.

Would you be okay with your friends picking who you marry? How about picking your career path, what your money will be used for, how you will spend your time, where you will live, and all the other big and small details? If you knew this was what was going to happen while you were lying there in a coma, would you be at peace or would you be worried?

Now, this is just a hypothetical scenario. You will never really find yourself in such a situation, at least not exactly like that. You see, this is actually what your life is like in reality; you might not have your friends choosing what you do explicitly, but they are definitely influencing your every decision. Because we are very social beings, we are very easily influenced by the world around us and tend to do what we think the people around us want us to do.

So even though you are not in a coma and unable to make any decisions, your friends are still influencing the decisions you make. If you were not comfortable with the idea of your friends making decisions for you for three years straight, then you should reconsider the friend group you have. The image that you had when you imagined what your life would be like if your friends made all of your important life decisions for you is still the life that you will have if you allow your friends to influence or have input on the decisions you make yourself.

This idea is not specific to only your friends, but it extends to all the other areas of your life in which you interact with people. Your family members and colleagues at work can also have an impact on how you make decisions and ultimately the person you become. In this chapter, we are going to explore how you can build relationships that are solid and will help you become the person you really want to be. We are going to go through some of the main pillars of strong and effective relationships and how you can foster those in your life.

Effective Communication Skills

The most important thing in any relationship is communication. If you do not communicate, then you might never figure out what the relationship's purpose really is and it may never reach its full potential. Communication is how you set the foundation of a relationship, and it is also how you keep the relationship going. If you do not communicate, you will end up with two different understandings of what the relationship is and how it is supposed to function.

The first way to promote and sustain positive communication in relationships is through active listening. The truth is that if you listen closely enough and for long enough, people will usually tell you what they want and what they are up to. The problem is most people do not listen very closely to the other person in a friendship or relationship. We hear what they are saying only to pick out what we want to hear, and then we respond and move on. This is why so many people say they feel lonely even if they have friends. It's because their so-called friends do not really take the time to listen to them.

As we discussed earlier, active listening is about involving yourself in the process when the other person is talking. You should have both your mind and body focused on what they have to say and encourage them to keep going until they are done. I know this is easier said than done now that we live in this digital world where we often feel the need to be on our phones all the time. But I promise, if you just take a few minutes to listen to your friends intentionally and wholeheartedly, you will be able to understand who they really are and what they want from the friendship.

The truth is that everyone wants something from every friendship or relationship they get into. We are all in friendships to use each other in a way. You might be in it for emotional support, advice, or experiences and memories, or you might be in it to learn something, but there is always some way we benefit from our friendships with others. In fact, if you gain nothing from being friends with the people you are friends with, then that is a cause for concern. So listen carefully to your friends when they talk, and maybe you will gain a better understanding of what they want and where they are going to take you.

If you fail to properly establish the purpose of the relationships in your life, you might end up being used by the people around you who know what they want. If you do not have direction, you will end up going in someone else's direction. This means you need to know who you are and what you are willing to give in a relationship. This is how you will find the confidence to be assertive and have strong, clear boundaries in your relationships.

When you become assertive and respectful, you become the type of person people actually want to be friends with because there is nothing more worthy of respect than someone who knows what their boundaries are and who will also respect yours. There is something about being assertive and respectful that will help you be honest and candid with your friends, and these are qualities that will help you stay in your lane even if it means losing some relationships.

It's okay to lose people if they do not align with the plans you have for yourself and your life. You are more important than all your friendships, so you must always put yourself first. Now I am not saying you should be selfish and take advantage of others for your own personal gain while you protect yourself from being exploited by others. However, you need to be in good mental and physical shape if you are going to make a real impact on the world. Because of this, the best way to be a good friend is by taking care of yourself so that you have the strength and ability to care for the people around you.

Building Trust in Relationships

Once you have communicated what you want from the relationship and have a good understanding of what the other person wants as well, it's time for you to build trust within the relationship. Trust is a state where you know that the intentions of the other person are in line with what they have communicated with you and you can therefore use that to judge what their actions will be. When you trust someone, you also judge their intentions based on your faith in their word all the time.

It's not easy to build trust—heck, you might have problems trusting family members who have been there all your life or people who have been on your side for years. It's very hard to build trust, but it is not impossible. The number one thing you need to learn in order to build trust with people you intend on growing with is consistency and reliability. You need to become the type of friend who is predictable and who always does what he says he will. People look for patterns to create mental frameworks and schemas. This means that if you are consistent and do the same things whenever you are faced with a situation, your friend's brain will tell them that that is who you are, and they will trust you to do that all the time.

If you show up for every meeting on time, you become that friend who they can always count on to arrive on time. If you are that friend who never forgets a birthday or who is always there to help in times of trouble, then that becomes who you are to your friends. You can use this to build the trust you want your friend to have in you but also as a standard for choosing who you can trust and to what extent.

I have found one of the markers of a good friend is someone who will protect you at all costs from the rest of the world. The most important way a friend can protect you is by keeping your sensitive information private. Since you spend time with your friends, you probably know a lot about them and their lives. Some of the things you will discover are embarrassing and may even tarnish your friend's image. Because you have this information and you are a friend, you have an obligation to keep it between yourself and your friend no matter what.

You are like a vault of secrets and personal information for your friend, and that is a role you should take seriously. You know you would not want to have your friends tell the world what they know about you, so do not do it to them. You do not protect your friends simply because they also know things about you that you want to be kept private. No, you do it because you are a good friend and you genuinely care about them.

Even when you fight with your friend or go your separate ways, you should never go back to what you know about them and use that as leverage on your friend. This will expose your character and give way to some very bad habits that will not be easy to shake off. This is how people can become conceited manipulators who only care about themselves and are willing to hurt others to get their way.

I want to end this section with a challenge for you. I want you to write down a list of all your close friends, and as you write each name, I want you to think about the type of friendship you have with them. You just need to get an overview of what you are both interested in and why you are friends. You should also add close family members and other people you are close to in your life so you can get the full picture.

I want you to write on a separate sheet of paper all the people you are friends with but you do not know why, and on another piece of paper, write down all the people you are friends with that you want to get closer to. You can then analyze these sheets to figure out how you want to continue with these relationships.

Conflict Resolution Techniques

It would be unfair to go over how to create strong and healthy relationships without going over how to heal and mend relationships when they break. It's inevitable that you will have differences in your relationships. This is true for everyone and all relationships. You will get to a time when you have disagreements with the other person and need to find a resolution.

While the pathway to a solution will be different for every relationship and situation, I will give you some guidelines that can help you patch things up and avoid falling into the same traps over and over again. Being a real man is being able to resolve conflict, not win the argument, so now let's see how you can do this and maintain the relationships that are helping to shape you into the person you want to be.

The first thing to do when conflict occurs is address it promptly and confidently. You need to realize that the conflict almost has a mind of its own, and its goal is to keep you separated from your friend. The longer you have been separated from your friend, the weaker your connection gets and the harder it will be for you to overcome the conflict you are facing. Think about it this way: If you are having a conflict because your friend was late for an event that meant a lot to you, you can talk to them about it and resolve it within a few days. On the other hand, if you become upset with them and do not talk for three months, you're allowing the issue to become bigger than it needs to be. It will eventually take up more of your energy than it would have if you'd made the effort to find a solution right away.

You should address the conflict as soon as you can and as boldly as you can. You need to show your friend that you understand that things are not well but that you want to work together to resolve the problem. You can be extremely angry at each other, but you still need to be on the same team as you fight to restore your friendship, and you should take the initiative to start working toward a solution.

The idea is not to get your way or make your friend understand you. The goal is to find a solution that accommodates both of you. You want a solution that will make both of you happy now but that will also help you avoid having the same issue again in the future. While you are resolving the conflict, show compassion to your friend and be understanding and accommodating.

Make an effort to understand the other person's viewpoint because that's the only way you can really start to resolve the issue. When it comes to most issues, the people involved generally want the same thing for each other in principle but do not always act in a way that reflects that. When you ask the two people what they want for the other person, their answers will probably be really similar, showing that there is no need to fight with each other in the first place and that a resolution is possible.

I know I said you should resolve conflicts as soon as they happen, and yes, that is the best-case scenario, but things will not always happen that way. In some cases, you can be so distraught in the moment that you won't be able to think straight enough to look at the matter objectively and make a fair judgment. In such cases, you will have to excuse yourself and cool off first. In some cases, you might be okay, but the other person might need space to cool off, and that's okay too. In fact, the ability to realize that your emotions are too high and you need to cool off before you attend to the conflict is a great first move.

After you leave to cool off, make sure you go back to resolve the issue as soon as you can. To be honest, even while you are away cooling off, you will already have begun to resolve the issue, and when you approach your friend, you will carry on with the collection of thoughts you have been working with in your mind.

Recognizing Toxic Relationships

Remember those friends we talked about in the introduction to this chapter? The ones who would not make the best decisions for you if they had to? Well, now it's time to learn to recognize them and start to cut those connections. You probably already have an idea of who those people are in your life from the exercise where you had to make a list of your friends, so in this section, we'll get a little deeper into that exercise.

There are three red flags that you should be able to spot and that you cannot ignore in a relationship: manipulation, emotional abuse, and control. These things can lead to betrayal and deception in relationships, and in most cases, there is nothing you can do to get rid of these negative traits in another person.

Manipulation is when the other person uses indirect tactics to control your behavior, emotions, and relationship. The most common way people will manipulate others is when someone plays the victim so they can push you into feeling like you have to play the hero and rescue them. This can easily turn into a cycle where you will always be the one helping and the other person only shows up when they need help. Manipulation can go beyond that though, and it's often so elusive that you might find it hard to pick out. This is when having many good friends comes in handy. If you do not see what is happening, maybe one of your other friends can point it out.

Control and emotional abuse are a two-for-one combo that will have you second-guessing yourself every time you do something with these kinds of friends. The problem is that emotions are very fragile, and you might have a hard time resisting the control that these friends have in your life because they use your emotions to make you feel obligated to do what they want. Basically, they convince you to do things you do not want to and show no regard for your boundaries whatsoever. In the next chapter, we will go over the idea of boundaries more to help you come up with some that can protect you from manipulation, control, and emotional abuse.

The people around you are going to be your support system as you go on this journey to embrace your masculinity and become a real man. It's important to make sure that the people you surround yourself with have the same idea of what it means to be a man and that they are supporting you as you grow into that. It will be much harder for you to win this battle unless you really narrow your circle of friends down to people who have the same trajectory as you.

As the saying goes, birds of a feather flock together, but some of the people you might be trying to move with may not even be birds. Maybe they are fish and have no intention to fly in the first place. Maybe they are snakes and you are actually prey to them. This is why you need to keep your eyes as well as your heart open and show grace, compassion, and understanding, but do not hesitate to cut off anyone who will hold you back from becoming the person you are destined to be.

Ninth Truth: A Man Who Values Trust and Wants to Create a Safe Environment for Everyone Will Respect Boundaries and Consent

It is important for you to learn to respect boundaries and consent because you do not own the world. So many men are under the illusion that because they have a responsibility to care for the world, they own the world. This is simply not so; you have an obligation to care for the world and the spaces that you find yourself in but only to the extent that you will not encroach on other people's private space.

This is the truth that will keep you from becoming what I call an unintentional bully. A lot of people become unintentional bullies, imposing their power and authority as if it has no limit and doing what they think is right in the moment. Part of being appropriately integrated into society is understanding that what you think is right isn't always what's right for everyone, and you need to be mindful of the people around you and respect what they say and how they feel, especially when it comes to their personal space.

Understanding Personal Boundaries

Everyone has walls around them, boundaries that keep them safe from the outside world. It's okay to have boundaries—in fact, you should have boundaries. Imagine if countries did not have borders; people would come and go as they pleased and there would be no sovereignty or sense of protection. Anyone could go anywhere and do whatever they wanted. This is not ideal for any state, and it is not ideal for you.

Personal boundaries can come in many forms, starting with physical boundaries. These are limits a person sets for how close another person can physically get to them before they feel uncomfortable. Some people will only be okay with a handshake and not want a hug, while others will give you a hug but then step away to maintain their boundaries. You can actually tell when you have invaded someone's personal space by the way their face changes, but we will talk more about that later.

There can also be emotional and psychological boundaries that individuals establish to protect their well-being and maintain autonomy. This is why some people do not talk about their personal lives to a total stranger or feel comfortable sharing their emotions with someone they do not know well. The idea is that everyone should be free to protect themselves as much as they want, and no one has the right to cross another person's boundaries.

I want you to learn to recognize when your boundaries have been violated so that you can assert your boundaries and set limits. Recognizing when your boundaries have been crossed will teach you to recognize when you have crossed other people's boundaries and how you can avoid doing so. Before we get there, though, I want to talk about what I call the rings of personal space.

Everyone has three rings around them that determine whether someone is in your public space, social space, or personal space. It can be hard to tell where each person's three circles begin and end because some people's circles are wider while other people's circles are smaller. First, we will talk about how you can figure out your own, and then we will talk about how you can protect them and keep them intact.

Think about the times you've been out in public spaces with a lot of other people. While in those spaces, you can pass by so many people and not even notice because they are in your public circle. You do not have to say anything to them and they may not even register in your mind. However, sometimes you might be standing in a line or sitting next to someone and suddenly feel like it might be appropriate to give them a nod or say hi. This is because they have just moved into your social space. Your social space is that place where you recognize people are there and feel like it would be rude to not acknowledge them. Last is your personal space. If someone enters your personal space, you may feel uncomfortable and try to move away.

The limits for personal space can change based on the situation. If you are in a packed elevator, someone standing shoulder to shoulder with you might just be in your social space while the same proximity outside might feel completely uncomfortable.

If someone gets closer to you than you are comfortable with, it's okay to assertively point it out. Stop, look at them, and say, "Would you mind moving back a little? You are in my private space, and it's making me feel uncomfortable." Never let people get into your personal space if you do not want them to. You always have the choice to say something about it.

If you fail to recognize and address when other people are in your personal space, you will also have a hard time recognizing when you are in other people's personal space and need to move out. You cannot respect for others what you do not respect for yourself. You need to practice setting and maintaining these boundaries for yourself, and then you will become aware of how your personal space interacts with the people around you.

It goes without saying that you will have different boundaries with different people. You need to define those as clearly as you can. If you think you are okay with cuddling with someone, you need to verify that the other person is okay with it as well. You should never assume that you have charmed someone enough to reduce the level of separation between you. If you have already started defining and holding people to your boundaries, then you know it can be hard for someone to push you out of their personal space if you invade it.

You cannot just assume that the other person is okay with you getting closer to them, putting your arm around them, giving them a hug, or even touching them at all. You need to pay attention and be aware of how that might affect them. There are signs that people will give off that will tell you when they are not comfortable with the closeness between the two of you, and you can use these to decide if the other person is okay with how close you are. Otherwise, it is always best to talk about it with the other person so you can make sure you are respecting their boundaries.

Setting Boundaries in Relationships

Just because you are with someone does not mean that there will be no boundaries between the two of you. In fact, if you are in a relationship with someone, the boundaries become even more important because not respecting them can lead to issues in the relationship or even the relationship failing altogether. You need to be very careful about how you manage your boundaries with the people you are in relationships with. This is especially important with romantic partners, but it's important with your friends and family too.

Setting clear boundaries will help you maintain respect and boundaries in your relationships, which will make them stronger. Just because you are close to your parents or best friend does not mean you can do whatever you want when you're with them or in their house. There should be limits to what you can do, and you should mutually agree on these limits.

I remember there was a time while I was in college when I would have visitors over to my dorm room, and I would have a whole list of requirements while they were there. I was very fussy about order and how things looked, so I had a space where the people who visited me could leave their bags, shoes, jackets, and so on whenever they came over. As soon as the visitors got in, I would tell them where to place their bags and everything else immediately. When I did not do this, the bags would end up on the floor or on the bed, and I would end up resenting the visit without even letting the other people know.

That is what happens when you start to invade the space of your friends, family, and romantic partners. They will slowly start to resent you because you make them feel uncomfortable by not respecting their boundaries. This applies to you as well; if your friends, family, and other people don't respect your boundaries, you may start to resent them, and this can affect your relationships with those people.

It's therefore important to discuss your boundaries and personal space with the people you are in relationships with as early as possible. The best way to have these types of conversations is to be as clear and candid as possible. I want you to set up a chat with your friend, family member, roommate, or whoever and tell them what you want to talk about ahead of time. When you meet, be ready to share your boundaries as well as ask them what theirs are.

Give them a chance to express their boundaries first. You can even help them by breaking down the areas into their personal space, belongings, physical space, and so forth. When they are done telling you what their boundaries are, then you can go ahead and tell them yours. Be as clear and precise as you can, and do not leave anything open-ended because your friends and family will not know what you're okay with and what you're not unless you tell them.

It is also important to conclude the conversation with an understanding that either party can reopen the conversation if there is something new that comes to mind or if something happens and they feel they need to adjust their boundaries. It's very important to be able to freely have this conversation when you need to, and you should make sure the other person knows that too.

Communication and Consent

Consent is the enthusiastic, informed, and voluntary agreement to engage in a particular activity or interaction with someone. In most social settings, consent is often implied and not necessarily written down or legally recorded. When you go out with your friend group, the assumption is that you have agreed to do all the activities that are part of going out, like eating and traveling together.

However, you may not always be on the same page with the other person. Sometimes you might think that you both have the same idea when in reality, the other person has a different understanding than you do. It is therefore very important to always explicitly communicate your boundaries and make sure that the other person expresses consent before you do anything with them. Some people are generally agreeable and will go along with you even when they do not feel like what you are doing is okay, and it is not okay for you as a man to take advantage of that.

In some ways, it's your job to make sure that you protect the boundaries and limits of the people around you. For example, if you go out with a girl and she tells you that she doesn't like drinking, you should not try to convince her otherwise. It's not your place to try and change her mind or talk her into having just one sip. Instead, you should keep that boundary in mind, and if at some point, you notice she is about to drink, you should check in and make sure she is really okay with it and not doing it because of peer pressure.

The crazy thing is when you show respect for other people's boundaries, they end up shifting those boundaries for you because they realize you are a safe space. If you try to bring down someone's walls by force, you are the reason those walls are there in the first place. You are the reason they avoid drinking when they go out with guys and the reason they would rather go home alone than with you.

If she says the date is over and that she wants to go home, you need to take her home without trying to make her feel bad about it. Remember, you do not own anyone or the world, and you are not entitled to anything, even if you want it or think you should be. Instead, you should dedicate yourself to helping meet the needs of others, and they will do the same for you. You are not owed an extra hour of dancing; you are not owed a hug, kiss, or anything else. If the other person clearly expresses that they do not want to be somewhere or do something, then that is it. You need to honor and support that.

From the many conversations I have had with other men, it seems the issue with consent and boundaries is really an issue with respect and humility. If you do not respect yourself, you will not be able to respect another person, and if you are not humble, you will not be willing to accept that someone would want something other than what you want. These are very dangerous characteristics because they blind you from what is really happening around you.

When you insist and lead someone to do something they have said they do not want to do, you might feel like you are completely irresistible and that they *want* to do whatever you tell them. In reality, this is not why that person chose to do whatever it was that you wanted them to. The other person might actually be feeling afraid, weak, ashamed, and powerless. When they say no, you might see it as a way to resist your charm when it's really just them genuinely expressing that they do not want to do something. You might see it as a challenge to try harder to convince them, and when this happens, you are ultimately coercing someone to do something against their will. You do not ever want to become such a monster. You need to remain compassionate and humble enough to accept when someone says no. It is not always about you, and oftentimes it's not about you at all.

Consider that they have a whole life apart from you that influences how they make decisions and what they're comfortable with. You are not there to help them figure out what is right for them; a real man will support what they say and want. If what they want happens to violate your boundaries and you are not okay with it, say so. You also have the right to express how you feel and walk away from situations that make you feel uneasy.

Even if you received consent at some point, this does not mean you have been given permission permanently. If a girl says yes to a kiss from you, that is all that yes is good for. In addition, it's only good the moment they agree to it. Look at it this way: Have you ever agreed to something? Maybe one night you ordered a pizza, agreeing to pay for it to be delivered. How would you feel if the pizza place started bringing you pizza randomly throughout the week and demanding payment?

It would be illogical of them to think that because at some point you wanted pizza and paid for it, you always want pizza and are willing to pay for it. It's the same with consent in relationships. If someone agrees to something at one point, it does not mean they have agreed to it forever. You cannot have sex anytime you want because they once said they wanted to. Instead, you need to check in every time and make sure the other person still feels comfortable.

In fact, you need to be able to accept and respect the other person when they take back their consent. If you are hooking up with a romantic partner and they end up changing their mind and asking you to stop, their consent has been revoked, and you need to stop immediately and respect the boundary. It's okay for someone to change their mind when you are already doing something with them. You could be driving to an event and they say they want to go home, and that's fine. It might be inconvenient, but you would want your change of heart to be honored if it were you.

Imagine if you were bound to everything you ever said or agreed to. As we grow and learn new things about ourselves and the world, we change our preferences and interests. It would be very stifling to be bound to a decision you made before you knew better.

Recognizing Signs of Consent and Non-Consent

Now let's go over how you can tell if someone is consenting or not from what they say as well as from their nonverbal cues. First and maybe most important is what the other person says. If you are with someone and they say they want to do something with enthusiasm, that is clear consent. If they say they want to try something but they are not sure, you should check in with them every now and then to make sure they are still okay with it. Do not try to push them into doing it just because they seem to have a hint of interest. Lastly, they might say no, and that is your clear sign to stop pursuing that avenue.

However, sometimes it can be harder to tell than that, and you need to look out for some nonverbal cues that might show you that the other person is not comfortable. There are so many of these, but here we'll talk about one of the more common ones.

The most common sign of non-consent is silence. If you ask someone if they want to do something and they do not say anything, do not take that to mean yes. "Simply put, enthusiastic consent means looking for the presence of a 'yes' rather than the absence of a 'no'" (RAINN, n.d.). It's not consent just because someone won't say no.

Being a man is a lot of things, but this is definitely one of the most important ones. The ability to respect others despite having the power to push them to do what you want is what it really means to be a man. A man's strength is not there so they can take what they want when they want it, as we covered in the first chapter. Rather, a man's strength is there to protect those who need it. I want you to make a promise from this day forward to stay alert to the boundaries of others and always seek consent before you do anything. In addition to that, I also want you to be aware of your own boundaries and protect them diligently.

Conclusion

Being a man is not easy, but that is part of what makes it worth it. It's a challenge that you have to willingly step up to. When you decide to become a man, you are voluntarily standing and choosing to face the chaos in your life and in the lives of the people around you. It's a selfless process that will require you to apply yourself, but one that will be rewarding if you are persistent.

This is not the end, however; it's only the beginning of your journey. From here, you will go out and try to apply these truths to your life as much as you can. You will fail every now and then, but learn something from your failures and get back up a stronger and more prepared person. That is what the journey will be like. Now that you know these nine truths of becoming a man, you can go out and see how far you can go. You will not be alone though. Remember that this book is like a guide and a friend, and it will be there to remind you of all the things we have talked about whenever you need it.

Every time you read through this book, you will find something new that you can apply to your life. In fact, I challenge you to read a chapter each month and try to spend that entire month applying the truth in everything you do. This will set you on a path to knowledge that will never end. By the time you get to the end of all nine truths, it will have been nine months, and you will have developed the mindset required to truly become a man.

True masculinity is a life lived in constant pursuit of what is meaningful and a dedication to protect, care for, and empathize with others. A real man does not seek to be served by all those around him; he is not power-hungry or glory-seeking but humble and ready to fight for the rights of those who need him. It might not always be the reward you expected, but there is something about chasing after honor and acting with integrity when you could do otherwise that rewards your soul. The peace you'll get from knowing your intentions are pure and your interactions are really aimed at creating better lives everywhere you go will always be enough compensation for a life lived helping others.

Now that you have seen how your life and mindset have changed from reading this book, I want you to think about what it could do to help improve someone else's life. You might know a friend or relative who is struggling to find their place in the world and needs to know the truths in this book. Well, share this copy with them, or if you can, gift them their own. I would love for the light that we have here to be spread to as many people as possible. Another way you can share your experience with this book is by leaving a review; maybe that will be the beacon for the next lost boy to pick it up and find their way as well.

Well done! I'm grateful you joined me on this journey, and I hope you enjoyed the read. Now it's time for you to live out the truths shared in this book in your own life. Bring your newfound knowledge to all your endeavors and relationships, and start writing your next chapter now.

References

Blake, K. R., & Brooks, R. C. (2022). Societies should not ignore their incel problem. *Trends in cognitive sciences, 27*(2). https://doi.org/10.1016/j.tics.2022.11.007

Christenson, K. (2021, February 1). *Assisting in personal hardships: The RTA program*. Nellis Air Force Base. https://www.nellis.af.mil/News/Article/2489470/assisting-in-personal-hardships-the-rta-program/

Dweck, C. S. (2006). *Mindset: The new psychology of success*. Random House.

Peterson, J. B. (2018). *12 rules for life: An antidote to chaos*. Allen Lane.

RAINN. (n.d.). *What consent looks like*. Rainn.org. https://www.rainn.org/articles/what-is-consent

Resilience. (2022, May 10). American Psychological Association. https://www.apa.org/topics/resilience

Young men. (n.d.). Beyond Blue. https://www.beyondblue.org.au/who-does-it-affect/men/what-causes-anxiety-and-depression-in-men/young-men#:~:text=One%20in%20seven%20young%20men

Milton Keynes UK
Ingram Content Group UK Ltd.
UKHW020756241123
433194UK00015B/806

9 798223 802822